Doing English

Aimed at students of English Literature in their final year of secondary education or beginning degrees, this immensely readable book is the ideal introduction to studying English Literature.

Doing English presents the ideas and debates that shape how we 'do' English today, covering arguments about the value of literature, the canon, Shakespeare, theory, politics and the future of the subject.

In his lucid and engaging style, Robert Eaglestone:

- orientates you, examining what it is to 'do English'
- equips you for future study, explaining key ideas and trends in English Studies in context
- enables you, bridging the gap between 'traditional' and 'theoretical' approaches to literature

Practical and provocative, the new third edition of this classic guide is fully updated, including new material on English, assessment objectives and a new chapter on creative writing.

Robert Eaglestone is Professor of Contemporary Literature and Thought at Royal Holloway, University of London, and Series Editor of *Routledge Critical Thinkers*.

D0061852

Praise for Previous Editions

'Excellent: a thought-provoking and accessible argument exploring the changing character of English Literature as it has developed outside the school curriculum over the last half century.'

The English and Media Magazine

'Exactly what students need.'

Times Education Supplement (for second edition)

'*Doing English* is an immensely helpful introduction to the academic transition from school to university ways of studying English. The sudden appearance of literary theory on the syllabus is only one of many ways in which the "subject" of English is reconstituted at this stage, and the first months can be very disconcerting. Eaglestone's clear and stimulating guide is exactly what students need to get their bearings.'

Peter Hollindale, *Times Educational Supplement* (for first edition)

'An excellent book, a very readable text of a fascinating and varied area of study that has repercussions beyond the lecture hall. *Doing English* is thoroughly researched and well discussed, appealing to scholars and students alike. If students in preparation for study of English at university level are to buy one book, let it be this one.'

Dr Delia Jarrett-Macauley, *Birkbeck College, London University*

'immediately accessible to any student approaching theory for the first time'

Dr Rosemary Pountney, *Jesus College, Oxford*

'*Doing English* does English proud. It's a sane and accessible view of how to study literature in its broadest sense. This is essential reading for students intending to study English to degree level – and for all those preparing for the challenges of new AS/A2.'

Adrian Beard, *Gosforth High School*

'an extremely useful guide to the subject'

Sue Dymoke, *The Secondary English Magazine (NATE)*

'A valuable, original book. I know of no other that prepares students for higher education in this way.'

Peter Childs, *University of Gloucestershire*

'a wonderfully clear account of what has been happening in the discipline of English'

Professor Brian Cox, CBE, *Chair of the North West Arts Board*

'This is a lively, intelligent but unpretentious guide to the current state of English Studies. In particular it seeks to bridge the gap between the English which A-level students experience and the subject which undergraduates encounter at university. Never could a book be more timely.'

Martin Blocksidge, *St Dunstan's College* and *Chairman of the English Association*

'a very good resource for A-level students and their teachers'

Clare Middleton, *Wheatley Park School, Oxford*

'This expanded third edition of Doing English provides an invaluable introduction to the constantly changing and vibrant world of English. Eaglestone's fluent thought takes his readers through the narrow by-ways of the subject and opens up the big picture. Engaging and thought provoking.'

Andrew Green, *Brunel University*

Doing English

A guide for literature students
(3rd edition)

Robert Eaglestone

Routledge
Taylor & Francis Group

LONDON AND NEW YORK

First published 1999
by Routledge
Second edition published in 2002
by Routledge
This edition published in 2009
by Routledge
2 Park Square, Milton Park, Abingdon OX14 4RN

Simultaneously published in the USA and Canada
by Routledge
270 Madison Ave, New York, NY 10016

*Routledge is an imprint of the Taylor & Francis Group,
an informa business*

© 2009 Robert Eaglestone

Typeset in Times by RefineCatch Limited, Bungay, Suffolk
Printed and bound in Great Britain by
TJ International Ltd, Padstow, Cornwall

British Library Cataloguing in Publication Data
A catalogue record for this book is available from the British Library

Library of Congress Cataloging in Publication Data
Eaglestone, Robert, 1968–
Doing English / Robert Eaglestone. – 3rd ed.
p. cm.
Includes bibliographical references and index.
1. English literature – Study and teaching (Higher) – Great Britain.
2. English literature – History and criticism – Theory, etc.
3. English literature – Outlines, syllabi, etc. I. Title.
PR51.G7E25 2009
820'.71'241 – dc22
2009019696

ISBN10: 0–415–49673–5 (hbk)
ISBN10: 0–415–49674–8 (pbk)
ISBN10: 0–203–09185–X (ebk)

ISBN13: 978–0–415–49673–5 (hbk)
ISBN13: 978–0–415–49674–2 (pbk)
ISBN13: 978–0–203–09185–2 (ebk)

Dedicated to my children, Alex and Isabella

Contents

Illustrations

Figures

Table

Acknowledgements

I've got a long list of people to thank for the third edition of this book, in addition to the ones I had to thank for the previous two. But mostly, I am grateful to the students I have taught on English courses at Royal Holloway, University of London (and some other places) for showing me how to do English.

Lots of people have read drafts and proposals and made useful comments that helped shape this third edition, so very many thanks to Carol Atherton, Pamela Bickley, Barbara Bleiman, Mark Currie, Naomi Harbidge, Tim Kay, Caroline Mills, Jenny Stevens and Gary Snapper, Jennifer Neville and Adam Roberts (both at Royal Holloway), and Sara Salih at Toronto.

I profited particularly from conversations about this book with present and former colleagues from Royal Holloway including Tim Armstrong, Jerry Brotton, Ewan Fernie, Elaine McGirr and Anne Varty. Douglas ('are you ready for some criticism?') Cowie deserves a special thanks for his help on the chapter on creative writing, as do Kristen Kreider and Sophie Robinson. I'd also like to thank the following for their support: Debbie Wheeler, Karen Kingsely, Marina Beck, Anna Sendall, Sarah-Jane Duval-Hall, Gaenor Burchett-Vass, Jean Rayner, Carol Eckersley, Jane Cowell and Daphne Pollen.

A third edition, too, has a history of editors. I am extremely grateful to Polly Dodson for her editorial commitment and enthusiasm. Thanks also go to her predecessors, Talia Rodgers and, especially, Liz Thompson, who edited earlier versions of this book with amazing understanding, passion and attention, above and beyond the call of duty. I'd like to thank Nikky Twyman for her work on the manuscript.

Thanks to the staff at the British Library (especially in Humanities 2), Senate House library, the Institute of Education library and the Royal Holloway library for being so unfailingly helpful.

Reading and writing books is also a social process (for me, anyway), so thanks to these people for their help and friendship: Phil Agulnik, Eva Aldea, Janice Allen, John Armstrong, Charley Baker, Mary Baker, Shahidha Bari, Adrian Beard, Oli Belas, Martin Blocksidge, Matthew Broadbent, Susan Brown, Peter Buckroyd, Rachel Carlyle, Nemonie Craven, Penny Crawford, Holly Crocker, Tommy Crocker, Maria Delgado, Sarah Dimmerlow, Simon Dowling, Cathy Dunkley, Mogs Eaglestone, William Eaglestone, Sarah Elgie, Viv Ellis, Jane Geere, Malcolm Geere, Sarah Geere, Judy Giles, Simon Glendinning, Tom Glennon, Sophie Goldsworthy, Nicole Gyulay, Tony Harris, Adrian Harvey, Nick Hoare, Alex Hollingsworth, Richard Jenkins, the Kelleys, Barry Langford, Henry Little, the Livseys, Sean Matthews, Sean McEvoy, Martin McQuillan, Tim Middleton, Robert Mighall, Nick Morwood, Ankhi Mukhergee, Alex Murray, Lawrence Normand, Sue Pitt, Rob Pope, Dan Rebellato, Ben Russell, Hilary Sanders, Danielle Sands, Helen Smith, Jenny Stevens, Gavin Stewart, Dan Stone, Richard Tennant, Sarah Tennant, Julian Thomas, Emma Townsend, Sally Twite, Nadia Valman, Zoe Van Den Bosch and Tom Webster, with a special thanks to Geraldine Glennon.

Introduction

- Who is this book for?
- What is it for?
- How to use this book

If you are studying English literature for AS/A2 level, for the International Baccalaureate or on an Access course, or are starting a degree in literature, this book is for you. In fact, whatever English literature course you are taking, no matter where you are, this book is not only an ideal stepping-stone to higher education but also an introduction to crucial new questions and ideas about English and literature.

In Britain, the University and Colleges Admission Service (UCAS) figures show that English is far and away the most popular Arts and Humanities subject. In higher education, only Business Studies, Computer Science, Design Studies and Law have more students. Despite being so popular, and perhaps rather surprisingly, there isn't a clear answer to the question 'What is English?' To say that it is 'the study of literature', 'analysing writing' or simply reading novels, poems and plays, and thinking and writing about them, doesn't really answer the question. What does 'learning about literature' or 'studying English' actually mean?

What ideas does it involve? Why do it one way rather than another? People usually set off 'doing English' without thinking about *what* they are doing in the first place and, perhaps more importantly, *why* they are doing it. The answers to these questions are vital because they shape what you actually do and how you react to the literature you study. While it sometimes looks as if English is simply the discussion of literature, it is a subject, or a *discipline*, and this shapes ideas that are often 'below the surface' or taken for granted and are not discussed. (It can be a bit of shock to think of reading and talking about books, something which seems very straightforward, as a discipline but the first three chapters of this book explain why this is.)

Although teachers of English at all levels in education have had long and tortuous debates about all these questions, these discussions – about how to do English, about the discipline of English – and their results have rarely been explained to you, the person who is actually studying English, even though they affect your assessments, essays and projects and even what and how you read. *Doing English* aims to explain these ideas and show how they influence you. It is for anyone who asks: 'When I'm doing English, what exactly am I doing?'

What is it for?

This book is an introduction to studying literature today. It is necessary because the study of English literature is constantly changing, and has changed almost beyond recognition in the last thirty years. This is not only because students of the subject now study more contemporary writers and can now often involve creative writing as part of studying English but also, and more importantly, because there has been a huge influx of new ideas into the discipline of English. One result of these changes is that there can sometimes be a large gap between doing English at degree level and doing English at secondary level.

So what exactly created this gap? This is one way to picture the changes in the subject of English: if you had gone into a large library thirty years ago you would have found shelves and shelves of novels, poems and plays. You would also have found a section of 'literary criticism', with studies on writers and their work. But, if you go into a big enough library today, you will also find a section called 'literary theory', which simply wouldn't have been there thirty years ago. This section – containing books on feminism, postcolonialism, postmodernism and all sorts of other subjects – is about new ways of doing English that have been taken up and used. These new ideas, often summed up as 'literary theory', created this gap, and doing English today means having a sense of what these ideas are and, crucially, *why* they have arisen.

Because of these new ideas, English as a subject has changed and become much more wide-ranging and exciting, and these changes have affected all of us who study or teach English. This book's aim is not to explain in great detail all the new ideas that make up 'literary theory', but to explain *why* they are studied to explain how a literary critic thinks. I believe that if you know *why* you are studying something, the subject becomes easier to understand. So, this book aims:

* *to orientate you*, by explaining what you are doing when you are doing English;
* *to equip you*, by explaining basic key ideas;
* *to encourage you*, to explore newer ways of doing English.

What are we doing when we are doing English? This question is important because so many of us study and teach English literature and it would be nice to know what it is we are supposed to be doing. It is also vital because people with very different views on politics, morals, religion, education, history and everything else have clashed time and time again over the subject of English, and these clashes have shaped the subject in particular ways. To think about English and how we look at literature is to see a reflection of these clashes, of ourselves and of our cultures. This idea is developed slowly throughout the book.

How to use this book

Often courses, exams and assessment seem to be more concerned with facts (whatever a 'fact' might be in English) than with ideas: people focus on dates, for example, and not *why* things happen. But this is a book about ideas and should be read in that light. For example, although I mention people throughout the book, what is important about them is not so much their names or dates, but the *ideas* they have had and passed on to others.

The book is in four parts:

* How we read

- What we read
- Reading, writing and meaning
- English studies . . . ?

Each part contains chapters that explore in detail one idea that is central for doing English today. The book finishes with a 'Further reading' section, which is broken down by chapter. This final section shows you where the ideas covered in each chapter came from and where you can read about them in more detail.

Each chapter starts with a list of questions and finishes with a summary highlighting the main ideas covered. A couple of chapters also have diagrams which expand on important ideas. The book is designed to be read in chapter order and gets more complex as it progresses. Since each chapter builds on the preceding one, you may prefer to read one chapter at a sitting and allow the ideas it raises to sink in before you start reading the next one. Or you may not. Having outlined how the book works and what it's for, I will now turn to the first question. Where did the subject of English come from?

PART I

HOW WE READ

1

Where did English come from?

- How is a subject made?
- How and why was English invented?
- How did 'modern' English evolve?

To understand why English is the way it is today, it's important to understand where it came from. Every subject we study is influenced by the history behind it, and English is no exception. Although it would be fairly straightforward to describe the invention of, say, a particular machine (the aeroplane, for example), the invention of a *subject* is much harder to pin down. This is because English is not a straightforward thing, but an *idea*. The evolution of any idea is intimately involved with other ideas, historical events, movements and the way people saw the world at particular moments in time.

The 'Chinese encyclopedia'

Subjects, or more formally 'disciplines', can seem like pigeonholes into which everything in the world is carefully placed. When we see an animal – a stray dog, perhaps – we know that the discipline that studies animals is 'zoology'; when we look out at the hills, we know that 'geography' studies them. And we could imagine that if we organised all these disciplines together into a huge encyclopedia, it would seem as if everything in the world had an encyclopedia entry to explain it.

But consider this account of a fictional 'Chinese encyclopedia' by the Argentinean writer Jorge Luis Borges (1899–1986):

Animals are divided into:

(a) belonging to the Emperor,
(b) embalmed,
(c) tame,
(d) sucking pigs,
(e) sirens,
(f) fabulous,
(g) stray dogs,
(h) included in the present classification,
(i) frenzied,
(j) innumerable,
(k) drawn with a very fine camel hair brush,
(l) *et cetera*,
(m) having just broken the water pitcher,
(n) that from a long way off look like flies.

The list is funny, but like the best jokes it asks some difficult questions that, when we think about them, might make us uneasy. For example, why do we find it funny? Because it seems so random? Certainly it offers a very different form of classification of animals from the encyclopedias in most of our libraries. More than this, it follows no basic organising principle that we recognise. And if every entry has a corresponding discipline, what would these be? From-a-long-way-off-look-like-flies-ology, perhaps, or Stray-dography. This looks like nonsense to us: our 'normal' encyclopedias use certain rules to select their entries and the corresponding disciplines seem far more sensible as a result. But are we taking too much for granted? How can it be that only our criteria and rules are valid? If you had learned about the world through this fictional 'Chinese encyclopedia', Stray-dography would make perfect sense, just as zoology does to us. This 'absurd' system makes us realise that although our system seems logical and natural, it too is made by people and therefore artificial. We use conventions to divide up our world, but really the world doesn't have set categories.

Subjects aren't natural, either; we invent them by dividing 'knowledge' up in a way that suits our view of the world. All of this suggests that disciplines are not just ways of studying things that already exist. Rather the categories we take for granted and the disciplines that study them are *constructed* and *reflect the world-view of those who construct them*. The category of 'literature' and the subject of English are no exception. They are closely linked with the way their inventors saw the world. Like every discipline, they developed through specific decisions, general trends and historical movements. Studying English as we do now would seem very strange indeed to somebody from the early nineteenth century.

With this in mind, and because they are still important today, I shall look at the decisions, trends and movements – usually not discussed – that shaped the discipline of English. This history tells us not only about the subject, but also about the changing ways in which people see and have seen the world.

The history of English

Some disciplines were invented long ago. Some scientists, for example, argue that people were doing what could be recognised as science in Egypt 2000 years ago and that the basic principles of scientific investigation (experiment, observation and conclusion) were formulated by the English philosopher and scientist Francis Bacon (1561–1626) around 400 years ago. Philosophy, too, can claim to have started more than 2500 years ago. In comparison, English, as we recognise it today, is a very new discipline. It started to emerge in the last decades of the nineteenth century but wasn't really established as a subject until after World War I (1914–1918).

This is not to say that people had not been writing about books until then: it's just that their writing was not recognised as serious investigation or as part of a subject in its own right. There was no subject that corresponded to the discussions people had about Shakespeare or the letters they wrote to each other about the books or poetry they had read. The study of literature in English simply did not exist. In fact, no one had even really discussed what 'literature' might mean: until relatively recently the term included what we would call history, geography, linguistics, biography, philosophy, sociology, politics, science and much more.

In the nineteenth century, the closest thing to what we know as English – and it was still pretty distant – was the study of the classics.

9

'The classics' were the ancient Greek and Roman plays, poems and texts from which British society drew a great deal of inspiration. The study of these were crucial in making one an educated gentleman. (And I do mean *man* – women generally weren't allowed to study them. In her *A Vindication of the Rights of Woman* (1792), the early feminist Mary Wollstonecraft (1759–1797) argued that the right to study the classics was vital for women's equality.) Most people thought that literature in English was at best an imitation of the classics and at worst only a mildly pleasant diversion. It certainly wasn't worthy of study in the way that the classics were. Academics considered the study of English literature – if it were to exist at all – should be for second- or third-rate minds (and, included in that, women). In 1887, Henry Nettleship (1839–1893), Professor of Classics at the University of Oxford, wrote a pamphlet called *The Study of Modern European Languages and Literatures in the University of Oxford*, which summed up the feelings of many people. He argued that the study of English literature simply could not be equal to the study of the classics: it could never be more than vague opinion and arty gossip. What was acceptable – just – was introducing English as philology, the science of language. If English were to exist as a subject, it would be as a rigidly scientific and historical study of the development of the English language from its origins to the present day. Without the scholarly rigour of philology, Nettleship believed that the study of literature was completely without substance, 'a phantom that will vanish at the dawn of day'.

However, if the study of English literature wasn't acceptable in Britain, and was of no use to professors of Classics, it was being actively pursued in the world elsewhere.

English and the British in India

During the first half of the nineteenth century, the British ruled India through a company called the East India Company, which had a complex contract or 'charter' concerning trade and the exploitation of territory that was agreed by Parliament and renewed every twenty years. In 1813 Parliament renewed the Charter, but made a number of changes. They increased the East India Company's responsibility for the education of the Indian population and at the same time made it much harder for the Company to support the work of Christian missionaries and preachers. Previously, the East India Company had helped to convert the Indian population, because the people in charge believed that Christian Indians would be more honest and hard-working, and more supportive of the Company's colonial exploitation. They thought that studying the Bible and Christianity made the population more 'moral', if moral is understood in the rather narrow sense of 'being in agreement with the principles of the Company'. However, many people in London thought it was quite risky persuading someone to become a Christian. (Perhaps this was because converting someone involved asking her or him a lot of searching questions, which Christianity then claimed to answer: the last thing Britain and the East India Company wanted was for anybody to ask searching questions about anything, in case their regime itself came into question.) The upshot of this was that the East India Company had to devise another way of making sure that the native population would be keen to follow an 'English way of life', at least enough to be good Company servants. The literature of England was seen as a *mould* of the English way of life, morals, taste and the English way of doing things, so why not teach Indians how to be more English by teaching them English literature? Studying English literature was seen as a way of 'civilising' the native population. By 1835, this tactic was made law by the English Education Act, which officially made English the medium of instruction in Indian education and required the study of English literature.

So it was in India, then, that the British formed the idea of a school and academic discipline called English, which involved reading and writing about novels, plays and poems written in English. This helps to explain why the subject is called 'English' and not, as in many other countries, 'Literature'. The idea that the study of English literature was a 'civilising force' remained very strong and it was this idea that brought the subject back to Britain.

English in Britain

During the nineteenth century, internal struggles threatened to tear Britain apart. There was a huge increase in population and the Industrial Revolution led to the growth of enormous cities filled with poor workers. Those in power felt that Britain was being overrun by these 'barbarians' and that anarchy or revolution was just around the corner. By educating the 'British savages' in 'civilised English' values, they hoped to maintain the political and social status quo. Many thinkers and reformers did feel that education was good in its own right, of course, but the hope of preventing revolution was certainly always in the background. Latin or Greek, considered the highest forms of 'civilisation', were assumed to be beyond the reach of almost everybody living in the slums of nineteenth-century Britain, whereas novels, plays and poetry written in English were not. The study of English literature was brought back to Britain to 're-civilise the native savages'.

The schools inspector, poet and thinker Matthew Arnold (1822–1888) is one of the most famous of these 're-importers'. In his best-known book, *Culture and Anarchy* (1869), he wrote that culture – and he means mainly literary culture – would make 'all men live in an atmosphere of sweetness and light'. We might see this as a little simplistic, but at that time many great hopes were pinned on English literature. Although there was no formal overarching subject that we would recognise as English, works in the language were taught on an informal basis. Often they were part of a mixed 'history' curriculum, taught in schools through the national universities extension movement, the National Council of Adult Schools Association and the Workers' Educational Association.

As the end of the nineteenth century approached, the discipline of 'English' as a study of literature didn't exist in universities or in any formal, extended way except as part of a broader subject in schools and adult education. Despite this, the teaching of English literature had become the focus of heated argument. On one side its supporters argued that it imparted beneficial and civilised moral values. One of the most influential of these campaigners, John Churton Collins (1848–1908), wrote a polemical book called *The Study of English Literature* (1891), in which he insisted that education, especially university education, had 'new duties and new responsibilities' to instruct people of all classes, not just the well off. Literature and the interpretation of literature, he claimed, could be taught to students of any background. For Collins, studying literature was a 'moral and aesthetic education', and had a positive and healthy influence on 'taste', 'tone', 'sentiment', 'opinion' and 'character'.

On the other side of the debate were those like Henry Nettleship, who thought that the study of English literature was of little worth, suitable only as a pastime for lesser minds. For such people, as I have outlined, only the historical study of the development of the English language was rigorous enough to count as a subject in its own right. Nettleship's pamphlet, *The Study of Modern European Languages and Literatures in the University of Oxford* (see p. 10) was published four years before Collins' book and was part of this debate.

For the most part it was the 'English as the study of language' point of view that triumphed. When Nettleship's own university, Oxford, introduced its first English degree course in 1893, it involved studying subjects like German, Old English and the history of the language. Poetry was a source of examples, and novels were not worthy of study. Interestingly, most of the students were women, which again fulfilled the sexist idea that English was for those 'less able' to cope with the great works of classical civilisation.

The situation remained like this for some time. Doing English mostly meant studying philology. However, two events were to change this radically and would introduce what we now recognise as English. The first of these events was the setting up of an English degree course at Cambridge University; the second, a government report.

How modern English began

In 1917, during the carnage of World War I, a group of lecturers at Cambridge University came together, planned and went on to introduce radical innovations in their university's (mainly philological) English degree course. This group, which included the now famous critics E. M. W. Tillyard (1889–1962) and I. A. Richards (1893–1979), wanted to create a subject that would study literature in English in its own right, not just as a source of examples of how English was used in Shakespeare's time, say, or as pale imitations of ancient Greek and Roman works. The intellectual inheritors of Arnold and Collins, they believed that the study of literature would restore a sense of humanity to the world, in the face of the rampant growth of technology, and the 'machine age'. The need for this, they claimed, was being graphically demonstrated by the ongoing world war. The programme they put together and the way they taught it reflected these beliefs and was to become hugely influential.

Two years later, the government commissioned a report with the aim of studying and suggesting improvements for the teaching of English in England. The Newbolt Report, finished in 1921 and named after the poet Sir Henry Newbolt (1862–1938) who chaired it, effectively gave government backing to this 'new English'. It stated that 'literature is not just a subject for academic study, but one of the chief temples of the Human spirit, in which all should worship'. In an imitation of the way

13

English had developed in India, according to the report a teacher of literature was no longer just a teacher like any other, but rather 'a missionary'. Indeed, as this rhetoric shows, the report thought that the study of literature for its own sake was practically a religious duty and literature itself almost a religion. Just as the teaching of English in India had replaced the government backing for Christian missionaries, so the discipline of English was, in part, seen as a substitute for the values and ideals that used to be taught through religion in Britain. The Newbolt Report was the final victory over those who wanted the subject to remain the study of the history of the language and increased the speed at which English as a discipline grew. It was vital in making this new form of English acceptable and laid the groundwork for the subject we recognise today.

Although there are many significant figures in the development of English, including the poet and critic T. S. Eliot (1888–1965), perhaps the most important for the 'new English' was the Cambridge University literary critic F. R. Leavis (1895–1978). He and his wife, Q. D. Leavis (1906–1981), did more to catch the mood of these changes and to shape what we think of as the discipline of English than anybody else. Both were early graduates of the new English degree course at Cambridge University and shared a number of very deeply held opinions about the state of modern culture and the role of English. Like the founders of the Cambridge English degree, the Leavises believed that the world was deteriorating: technology and industry were ruining humanity and human values, religion was dying, communities were falling apart. They felt that the modern world turned vital things and deep feelings into crass, coarse and trite popular clichés. In a number of very influential studies, such as *Mass Civilization and Minority Culture* (1933), they argued that only literature, and the rigorous study of literature, could remind us of our human values and of what was truly important. Works by F. R. Leavis, like *New Bearings in English Poetry* (1932), *Revaluation* (1936) on English poetry and *The Great Tradition* (1948) on the novel, are perhaps the most significant influence on how English literature was understood in the twentieth century.

The Leavises, always outsiders even at Cambridge University, committed themselves, with quite astonishing vigour and dedication, to establishing the study of English in a way which reflected their ideas. They became the leading figures in a prominent group who shared their opinions and who published a monthly journal, *Scrutiny*, which lasted from 1932 to 1953. Perhaps most importantly, they were not just enthusiastic teachers, but teachers of teachers: they passed their ideas down to younger generations, who became schoolteachers, examiners, journalists and so on. Many English teachers can trace a 'family tree' of teachers back to the Leavises or those directly influenced by them.

The 'Leavis method'

One of the Leavises' key achievements was to foster a particular approach to the study of literature and to demonstrate their method in their works of criticism. The key ideas of the Leavises and those they influenced ('Leavisites'), although never actually codified, can be roughly summarised as follows:

- The study of literature has a *civilising mission* to 'humanise' people and provide values which, in the modern world, can't be obtained elsewhere.
- For the Leavises, the aim of criticism should be to make an authoritative and *objective judgement* or 'evaluation' of a literary text. This means that your personal 'gut' response and views don't really count. You might say 'the play is flawed because . . .' or 'this character is engaging because . . .' rather than writing 'I don't like this' or 'I like this character'. Writing in the third person ('he/she/the reader') rather than the first ('I') is assumed to be more objective.
- At the same time, the reader must demonstrate *sensibility* or an individual response to the text which happens 'naturally' when a literary text is read. This idea relies on a belief that every person must have something in herself or himself that is capable of being moved by reading literature and the thought that English as a subject can draw out and improve this 'sensibility'.
- *Practical criticism* is the most effective method for studying literature. This form of reading, sometimes known as 'close reading', involves the intense scrutiny of a piece of prose or poetry, concentrating on the words on the page and disregarding the work's context. This is seen as an objective and almost scientific way of reading literature.
- There is a *canon* or authoritative list of great literary works that everyone with sensibility should study and admire. Authors like Geoffrey Chaucer, William Shakespeare, Jane Austen, George Eliot and Henry James would be included in the canon.

- A literary text is free from history and time, and has *intrinsic artistic worth*. The value is in the text and to do with the artistry of the text – we do not read because a text might tell us about, say, history or the author's life.

Many of the Leavises' ideas continue to shape the study and teaching of literature in schools, colleges and universities. You might even take some of these ideas for granted yourself, without knowing where they came from. This once radical way of studying English became so dominant for so long that many people thought you were only doing English if you had the same aims as the Leavises, and followed their approach. Challenges did come, however. The following chapters focus on these challenges, why they came about and how they have changed English as a subject.

Summary

- Subjects are constructed according to our world-view, so subjects change – or, in the case of English, come into existence – as our world-views change.
- Education in English literature began as a way of teaching 'civilised', 'English' values to the population of colonised India early in the nineteenth century. Later in the century this idea was applied to workers and others in industrialised Britain.
- The earliest English degrees in Britain concentrated on the study of language (philology), as the study of literature was not thought to be rigorous enough in its own right.
- During and after World War I, many thought that the study of literature would restore a sense of humanity to the world. In 1917, a group of Cambridge academics changed their degree programme and set up the study of English literature in its own right. A government report – the Newbolt Report – supported this 'new English' and encouraged its growth nationwide.
- Two of the earliest graduates of this Cambridge University degree, F. R. and Q. D. Leavis, led the development of English as we know it today. The Leavises' ideas about studying literature remain at the heart of much English teaching: a 'civilising' mission; objective judgement; personal sensibility; practical criticism; the canon; a sense of intrinsic artistic worth.

2

Doing English today

- Why did English change?
- What do these changes mean?
- What is 'literary theory'?
- What does this mean for you, doing English?

In the last three decades, there has been a revolution in English studies: teachers and students challenged the 'traditional' approaches to English and argued that there are other important ways of reading and studying literature. These new ways of reading are lumped together, perhaps rather unhappily, in the term 'literary theory'. But why have these changes taken place?

Changing world-views, changing English

English has been linked to the view that people need to be 'civilised' and provided with values through the study of literature. Looking at the development of English in Chapter 1, it is clear that this idea was intended, subtly but firmly, to force people into a single *mould* of 'civilised Englishness'. However, the world in which we live now is not the same world that the Leavises and others who shaped the subject lived in. Where the founders of English wanted people to be similar, now we appreciate and celebrate difference. Where they offered certainties and definite answers, we are aware that there are rarely clear-cut solutions and final judgements. We are much less sure about many things that they took for granted. And if our world-views are changing, so must our expectations of English. These changes are most clearly explained and explored by looking at the crucial issue of *interpretation*.

Understanding the changes: reading and interpreting

Understanding literature isn't a natural process: it doesn't just happen. We 'do' something when we read, we use certain tools to find meaning in a text, whether we realise we are doing so or not. What you make of a novel, poem or play is exactly that: what you *make* of it. Another way of expressing this is to say that to read a literary text, to think about it, or to write about it in any way, is to undertake an *act of interpretation*. When you interpret a text it means that you find some things important and not others, or that you focus on some ideas and questions and exclude others. Rather than reading in a vacuum, we take our ideas, our tendencies and preferences – *ourselves* – to a text. This means that 'reading' and 'interpreting' mean almost the same, and you'll see I use the words almost as synonyms in this book. It is because of the importance of interpretation that I have used the word 'text' regularly throughout this book. Apart from being shorter to write than 'novel, poem or play', it emphasises that reading is an act of interpretation – texts are things that are interpreted. (The word 'text' also makes it clear that it's not only literature that is interpreted; so are people's actions, television and music, for example. News is interpreted both when it is watched, heard or read, and when it is put together by journalists. All these are 'texts'.)

Because interpretation doesn't happen in a vacuum, *no interpretation is neutral or objective*. Whenever you interpret a novel, poem or play (or anything else for that matter: TV soap, advert, film facebook status update), your interpretation is shaped by a number of *presuppositions*. These are the 'taken for granted' ideas, tendencies and preferences you carry with you and, like glasses that you can't take off, you always read through them. On a surface level, your interpretation will be affected by the *context* in which you read and the *expectations* you have of the text. For example, if you read a novel about World War II for a history project, you'll think about it in a different way from how you would look at it if you were to read it for fun. At a deeper level, you bring with your presuppositions about yourself, other people and the world, presuppositions you may take so much for granted that you don't even realise you have them. At this level everyone has different presuppositions because – simply – people are different, to a greater or lesser degree, and have been shaped by different experiences. People from different backgrounds, sexes, sexualities, religions, classes and so on will be struck by different things in any text. Everything you have read and experienced previously affects how you interpret now. This idea can be summed up by saying that everyone is 'located' in the world. Just as you can't jump higher than your shadow, you can't escape your location in the world.

What do these ideas mean for the traditional 'Leavis method' approach to literature?

- English has a *civilising mission*.
  BUT: This 'civilising' appears to be a process of forcing people into a fixed pattern of values, ideas and opinions – a pattern of 'Englishness'. The world has changed and this ambition now looks thoroughly questionable.

- A novel, poem or play can and should be studied and *judged objectively*.
  BUT: No interpretation is objective. No judgement could actually be neutral, unaffected by your own presuppositions.

- The reader must demonstrate *sensibility*, a natural response which just 'happens' when a text is read.
  BUT: There is no 'natural' response to literature. The very fact that English is taught seems to confirm this. Moreover, the idea of sensibility implies that if you are not moved by a certain work of literature you have somehow failed. But who decides what should move us, and in what way? Their judgement cannot be neutral.

- *Practical criticism* is an objective, almost scientific way of reading literature.
  BUT: There cannot be an objective way to read literature, as every reader brings her or his own presuppositions to a text. This is not to say we shouldn't read closely, but to admit that, unlike an experiment which should reproduce the same result each time it is performed, each reading by each individual produces a different result.

- There is a *canon* of great literary works which everyone should admire.
  BUT: This assumes that judgements of worth could be neutral and disinterested.

- We read for the *intrinsic artistic worth* of a literary text.
  BUT: Who judges this worth? Doesn't context affect what is thought of as 'artistic worth'? The judgement of intrinsic worth depends on an external context.

As you see, this 'Leavis' way of approaching literature takes a lot for granted: that we think, read and make judgements in the same way or, more strongly, that we *should* think, read and make judgements in the same way. It is patently clear that those who invented this approach to English were influenced by their view of the world: if everyone was the same ('English'), there would be only one valid way of reading. If we were to express this in a diagram, it might look like this:

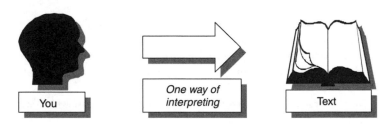

Figure 2.1 **The 'traditional' method**

Although the 'Leavis method' claims not to be a method, but rather to be objective and natural, when we look at it in detail we see that it clearly is a method and one that still carries a lot of weight. You might be able to see strong traces of it in your own English courses, or in discussions about literature in the media. However, as I've outlined above, its assumptions are very much open to question. It is this process of questioning in the discipline of English that has led to the growth of what is called 'literary theory' over the last thirty or so years.

What is 'literary theory'?

New ways of reading, grouped together under the term 'literary theory', are now seen as central to university English courses. A survey carried out by the Council for College and University English of all university English departments in the United Kingdom revealed that four out of every five taught a compulsory first-year course on literary theory. Three-quarters thought that knowing about literary theory was essential; the remainder thought it to be desirable. *But what is it?*

Literary theory is a catch-all term for a huge range of new and different ways of reading and interpreting texts. More correctly, then, it might be called 'literary theories', since different approaches needn't agree with each other. Moving on from the 'one right way' of interpreting, these new approaches to literature reflect the different concerns and ideas of a very wide range of people, not just a (so-called) 'cultured' English elite. This means that ways of reading which were marginalised or seen as 'wrong' because of the influence of the one, traditional model of English have begun to emerge and develop. Important and influential ideas from other disciplines have entered the subject: English now draws on subjects like history, politics, women's studies, sociology, gender studies, linguistics, philosophy and so on. As you begin to explore literary theory you will no doubt hear about historicism, cultural politics, feminisms and other 'theories' that have come out of these other disciplines. New ways of reading have also developed from within the subject of English itself,

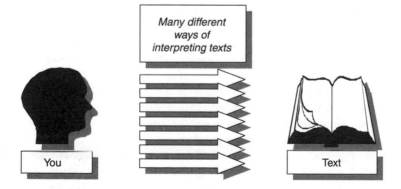

Figure 2.2　**Different ways of interpreting**

in reaction to the rather narrow focus of the traditional approach to literature.

These changes are most clearly seen if we redraw Figure 2.1 to represent the new view of 'doing English' (see Figure 2.2, p. 21).

At the heart of literary theory, then, is the realisation that every way of reading brings with it presuppositions. More than this, because everyone is different there simply cannot be one correct way of reading. But how is literary theory useful?

Using theory

This way of understanding what English is, and of understanding what you are doing when you are doing English, brings literature closer to you, the student. Those who have shaped English as a school, college and university subject have usually tried to teach about literature, art and life without admitting that the method they use takes certain ideas for granted. Often, they do not even show that English follows 'a method', assuming instead that it's 'the only way'. This often means that what you write in exams and essays about a work of literature has nothing to do with what you might really feel or think about it, which can be confusing and frustrating. To state this in formal terms, this shows the discrepancy between your location in the world and the presuppositions of the discipline of English. New approaches are trying to give more weight to different presuppositions and different ways of interpreting.

Once you've realised that interpretations are determined by world-views and that many interpretations are valid, you can begin to explore a whole array of important ideas. A key to this is remembering that you aren't limited to your own world-view: you can learn about different ways in which different people might interpret the same text. While your initial reading might be shaped by your presuppositions, literary theory offers a huge, possibly infinite, number of ways of approaching literature. You are free to choose one or another critical method, or to switch from one to the other, or to experiment with a selection. English becomes a question of reading certain sorts of texts in many different sorts of ways. There is no longer a '*right*' way to interpret literature.

What are the actual mechanics of using different approaches to literature? Any critical method works by reading with certain questions in mind. The context in which we read, our expectations and experiences, make us concentrate on certain issues when we read. These focus our reading and so structure our interpretations. For example, imagine the context for reading is that you have to answer an essay question and your expectation is that the material you need is in the text. Think about any of the novels, poems or plays you've studied. Now imagine you are asked any of these questions before you start to read: What happens in the plot here? Is this character likeable? How are metaphors being used to achieve a certain effect? Each of these three basic questions will draw your attention to different parts of the text: the plot question will make you look at events, the character question makes you concentrate on what that character says and does, the question on metaphor makes you look at how the language is woven together. By focusing your attention on different aspects of the text, the questions make you read in a different way and so lead you to different interpretations of the text. You might even play down metaphor or plot if you are concentrating on character.

Literary theories simply offer different sorts of questions to take into a text. Feminist approaches, for example, might suggest you ask: How does this text represent the relationships between women and men? Historical approaches might lead you to ask: What is this text telling us about its historical period? The text may or may not explicitly be about these things, but you make these questions your specific focus in reading and base your interpretation on them.

You can also think about the questions that shape other people's interpretations. If you're listening to a teacher or lecturer, or reading somebody's thoughts on a work of literature, ask yourself: What unspoken questions is she or he answering? By uncovering these questions, you will learn a lot about that particular method of interpretation and about what that person thinks is really important. A greater challenge is to ask yourself what questions haven't been answered, or haven't even been raised. Once you've worked through this, you can read the text with different questions in mind, and see how different critical methods give different interpretations. Each will show up things the other methods don't.

There's no need, incidentally, to think that all these theories will agree with each other; in fact, they are more stimulating and productive when they don't. Moreover, they don't add to a 'super-theory' or a 'Grand Unifying Theory of Everything'. Each has its own way of interpreting. Indeed, to have lots of different critical approaches to texts means that we can compare and contrast them. If English is about reading texts in different sorts of ways, it is also about examining how and why we choose these ways. English is not only about *reading* and enjoying literature; it's also a question of *thinking about how we read*. We can show this on our diagram, by adding another arrow representing a focus on interpretation itself. The name for this 'study of interpretation' is *hermeneutics*, which is what I've called the arrow in Figure 2.3.

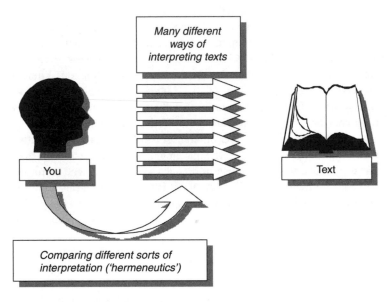

Figure 2.3 Doing English today

The realisation that how we read is as important as what we read is perhaps the most important innovation in the study of literature in the last twenty or thirty years. It has changed English completely as a subject and given it a new burst of life. And it is this realisation that underlies the new ways of reading that are called, in a rather all-inclusive way, 'literary theory'.

What does this mean for you?

Studying English involves not just reading works of literature, but learning to interpret them in different ways. It also involves understanding how different ways of interpretation work, as this can reveal what other people consider to be significant about literature and central to their lives. This has the potential to create exciting new readings of texts, but also to make you think about the way you see the world and your place in it. Consciously reading from different perspectives can change your ideas about the text and even about your place in the world. In this way, the subject of English can bring to light and even challenge ideas we take for granted. Because of this, many critics and educators say that this sort of questioning and reading from other perspectives is central to doing English and to the enjoyment of reading. I would argue that this power to make us think about ourselves and others is one of the things that makes English such a valuable subject and is why literary theory is essential to doing English.

Unfortunately, change doesn't come easily. The issues raised by literary theory have caused terrible arguments and divisions between students and teachers of English in schools, colleges and universities all over the English-speaking world. In part, this led to the gap between English in secondary and higher education that I discussed earlier. Although the situation has changed in English in the last few years, many students trained in the traditional method of studying literature continue to search for 'the right answer'.

Summary

Doing English involves reading works of literature, learning to interpret them in different ways and understanding how these different approaches work. These new approaches have the potential to create new readings of texts and to make you think about the way you see the world and your place in it. You are, or should be, free to choose one or another method, or to experiment with a selection.

- English as a subject is constantly changing. These changes can be understood by looking at the issue of interpretation. When you read, you interpret. No interpretation is neutral or objective, as we are all influenced by a number of presuppositions.
- 'Literary theory' is a catch-all term for a huge range of new and different ways to read and interpret texts, reflecting the different concerns and ideas of a very wide range of people, not just a 'cultured', 'English' elite. All this encourages us to think about how we interpret.

- 'Theory' also encourages us to contrast and study different methods of interpretation in their own right. This is called hermeneutics, the study of interpretation itself.
- How we read is as important as what we read.

3

English and 'the right answer'

- Is there a 'right way' to do English?
- What's wrong with the idea of having a 'right answer'?
- So how do I 'do English' in other ways?

It is often said that there is 'no right answer' in English. But coursework and essays are marked, authorities on literature are deferred to and exam answers revised, so it looks as if everybody secretly assumes that there really is a right answer. Why are students and teachers of English caught in this contradiction? And what are the consequences?

Is there a 'right way' to do English?

As I suggested in Chapter 2, it used to be assumed that you could read literature in a 'natural' way, as if you had no presuppositions. This natural, 'right' way would produce the 'right' interpretation of the text, in other words, 'the right answer'. This idea is still quite widespread. In many cases, it seems that the new 'theoretical' ways of approaching literature, with questions about presuppositions and context, are seen as 'add-ons', to be learned after you've mastered the 'natural' method of interpretation.

However, the traditional way of interpreting literature was, in fact, a sophisticated and complex system, with its own presuppositions and methods, all of which had to be learned. Students who 'did English' in this way had to learn to operate this complex system, to look through these eyes, in order to succeed. This was made harder because this system pretended not to be a system but 'common sense'. For example, this traditional approach used words that sounded ordinary and not like technical literary critical expressions: one of the Leavises' favourite terms was 'life'. They would say that literature expresses 'life', that great literature is 'life-affirming'. Other terms of praise were 'strong', 'direct', 'intense' and 'concrete'. In contrast, not-so-good works were 'weak' or 'brittle'. But this seemingly innocent language was as unnatural and impenetrable as any jargon until you had been taught what it means. The words 'life' or 'strength' are *technical* terms in this context and not 'common sense' at all. But at the same time as learning the terms, students learnt that to use them meant that they were 'doing English' the right way and coming up with the 'right answer'.

What's wrong with 'the right answer'?

In all sorts of education systems in all sorts of places, the search for 'the right answer' continues, and you may be doing a course where you feel as if this sort of 'answer' will get you good grades. This approach to literature can lead to a wide variety of problems, however. A good way to examine the consequences of these ideas is to look at the UK's old 'A-level' examinations. For those readers not familiar with the system, this was a two-year course, examined in the final year of secondary education. In 2000, the 'old A level' was replaced by two one-year courses, AS and then A2. (If I am turning back to the 'old' system, then, it is not to criticise teachers or examiners, but to show a fairly recent example of what can go wrong with an approach which assumes a 'right answer'.)

In the late 1980s and 1990s, much was written about the A level in relation to the problems of the 'common-sense approach' and the 'right answer'. Patrick Scott, a writer on education and at the time an A-level examiner, analysed these ideas in a book entitled *Reconstructing A-level English* (1989). He offered a particularly clear analysis of the results of learning this 'right way'. He began by noting that different A-level candidates from different boards, doing different syllabuses and sitting different papers, 'make strikingly similar mistakes'. Why? Because there is 'common heritage of teaching about literature which is actively disabling'. This common heritage is the idea of the 'right way'.

Here are some of Scott's examples of how this common heritage affected students (and might, perhaps, still affect you).

- It was taken as read that the 'author – any author – having selected a *theme*, then decorates it with a variety of *effects* that will make it *interesting* to the reader'. The student then had to 'unearth' that theme. This simplistic presupposition was so widespread that Scott cites an examiner who writes that many candidates 'simply did not know what to do with a poem that had no "message" or "moral"'. Students, he is saying, were taught that the only approach to literature is to look for a message or moral, and they could not cope if there was not one to be found.
- It was assumed that all readers interpret a text in roughly the same way. This was often signalled by the word 'we', in phrases like, 'When we read this masterpiece, we feel . . .' But what if you didn't feel the same way? Instead of being friendly and inclusive, this 'we' was often coercive and exclusive and, as Scott writes, it created

    a sense of dislocation between the individual and the book they have read. It introduces an army of other readers, all marching in time to the music [which implies] that texts have only one meaning and that critical disagreements are simply the way we get there.

- There was an assumption that judgements 'about complex literary texts . . . can be captured in one or two well chosen phrases' suggesting that a text is 'a seamless and consistent whole'. In fact, works are often contradictory or fragmentary or, famously in the case of *Hamlet*, have been made to *seem* consistent. How could you say one right thing about a text which doesn't say one thing itself?
- Scott also points out that students quickly discovered 'that not only do members of their A-level group disagree with each other, but so do eminent critics'. However, despite this, teachers and examiners 'will be expecting students to adopt a more "objective" analytical approach, the implication being that only in this way is it possible to establish what a book "means"'. It seems that if a student disagreed, or if any critic disagreed, it was because they were being too subjective.

However, the idea of 'objectivity', as I have shown, is very questionable.

- Because of this traditional approach, the texts studied became 'a category of book about which literary questions are asked and literary answers provided'. No longer just books, they are 'course books'. Because they are now in a 'special category', Scott argued that a student's 'previous experience of reading is no longer of value' and that they had to learn to read in 'an A-level way'. This meant learning to share – or pretending to share – the presuppositions of teachers and examiners. It is no wonder course books often seemed hard to read.

These assumptions and others were intensified by the examining process and by the curriculum. It is no secret that all A-level questions were about one of the following: theme, style, setting, character or plot. Study aids, which acutely pick up on the demands of A level, also reflected and so reinforced these presuppositions.

This split between what English claimed to be doing (inviting you to respond to a text) and what it actually did (teaching you to respond in one particular way, corresponding to one set of presuppositions) had a number of consequences. Perhaps most importantly, this 'split' made a personal response impossible and often discounted a student's own experience, ideas and presuppositions as 'wrong'. Scott writes that students became 'inhibited about trusting their own response' and instead discovered 'that the apparently open examination questions conceal a hidden agenda'. English A level was excellent at creating a 'reading machine' out of parts passed down to students, so that eventually they would 'manage to transform each set book into a collection of notes that will see them through the exam'. In the end, Scott suggested, students learnt to speak two different languages in response to texts: an 'A-level language' about the 'course texts' and an altogether different language to respond to – to criticise – the books and poems read, the films and TV watched, the music listened and danced to in their free time (and now websites visited, blogs written and read, and so on). Perhaps even more discouraging was the fact that, because students were being given conflicting messages about what to do, the subject seemed much harder than it should. Scott argued that sometimes the only way students could 'reconcile these conflicting versions' was 'by seeing it all as quite unmanageable'. The only other option was to see it as 'nonsense'. Most students, Scott suggests, 'if forced to decide whether "Eng. Lit." is nonsense or hard, will plump for it being hard'. He adds, mischievously, 'the notion that it might be nonsense is actually much more threatening'.

The assumption that there was a 'right way of doing English' was not only bad for students, but also for teachers. Many teachers – rightly, I think – treasure the idea that English is not like other subjects: it aims to encourage freedom and personal response, understanding and sensitivity. Perhaps even more ambitiously, some teachers have felt that English as a subject has a mission to make people more free and fulfilled in their lives and choices. Yet they often felt confined by the assumptions of a select group from the first half of the twentieth century, preserved in educational formaldehyde. Worse than just memorising facts, to be good at English students were forced to 'take for granted' a very different set of attitudes and ideas. Teaching events like videos, summer schools, performances, visits by actors and so on often showed how texts could be exciting and relevant. But if the bottom line was the exam, in the traditional mode, then much of this was wasted. This left many teachers frustrated and angry. But, oddly, the idea of a 'right way' was also bad for examiners and assessment. Not only do examiners get very bored with marking the same old predictable answers, but also they would have been aware that the basis of the exam was contradictory. Although they were supposed to reward candidates who offered well-thought-out answers that analyse and evaluate the text, it seemed as if the only answers that scored marks were the ones that produced the 'right answer' following the 'right way'. As a result, the examiners could not reward individuality, creativity or different approaches because the 'right way' is not individual or creative. And how could they tell real understanding from somebody parroting what they were 'meant' to say? If all the answers are based on the same presuppositions, then, in fact, they say the same thing. So, in the end, the examiners ended up marking not what a student's answer said, but how fluently they said it.

So how can I 'do English' today?

In the light of these problems, and in response to the growth of the other ways to interpret texts, there have been many changes in how English literature is studied, taught and examined: doing English has changed. In educational systems around the world and at a variety of levels, courses have changed to allow for a shift from 'traditional' to 'newer' approaches.

To begin with, the changes mainly occurred in universities and are now reaching secondary schools. To return to the UK example, I have suggested that one of the main problems with the A level was that there was generally assumed to be one right interpretation of a literary text. This meant that 'we all knew' what we were doing when we were doing English, but that the presuppositions were never made explicit. There was little guidance – except in the idea of the 'right way' – as to what students were supposed to do.

In response to this, the QCA (Qualifications and Curriculum Authority; a body who set the guidelines for exams in the United Kingdom) reviewed the examining system in 2000 and again in 2008. They not only replaced the two-year A level with the one-year linked AS and the A2 courses, but also introduced for all subjects a new set of 'Assessment Objectives' (or 'AOs'). These are sort of 'ground rules' for what is expected from you. In English Literature, there are four AOs. Teaching focuses much more clearly on these AOs than it did before. These offer more explicit criteria than the earlier A-level in English that involved absorbing and reproducing a set of unquestioned and unspoken assumptions. And, crucially, all the new AOs for English Literature introduce some of the basic ideas behind the newer literary 'theories'. As an AS or A2 student you now have to use 'appropriate terminology'. Some formal or technical language is always necessary; just as it is easier to say 'carburettor' than 'thing that mixes air and fuel in a car engine', it's easier to say 'Restoration Comedy' than 'that type of light-hearted play popular in the second half of the seventeenth and early eighteenth centuries'. You have to demonstrate 'detailed critical understanding' of the structure of a text and be 'informed by the interpretations of other readers'. You also have to demonstrate an understanding of the 'contexts in which literary texts are written and received'. 'Context' here means both the historical background and reception of the literary text at the time of its creation, but also how the text is seen today, in its (and our) current climate. Many texts – for example, those that deal with ideas about race, gender or politics – look very different now from how they did fifty or a hundred years ago. But the key point of these two objectives is to stress that it is not only possible to explore a range of different interpretations, but that you *should* explore them.

In all, then, the Assessment Objectives set up guidelines for what, in this context, is a good – not a right – answer. If you're not an AS or A2 student, it might be interesting to think about the ways you are being taught and examined, and to compare the 'ground rules' with those used here. Although the traditional approach to literary criticism seemed to suggest that 'you can say what you want as long as you can support it', in fact, it discouraged this. First, learning to support a 'non-conventional' argument, you need material and ideas that are rarely provided precisely because they aren't conventional. For example, you would find it hard to write an essay offering a psychological interpretation of one of your course books, if you had never been told what such an approach might involve or even that such an approach existed. Second, the way you are taught to argue relies on presuppositions, which you end up taking on board without even realising you are doing so. Is it a surprise that class after class of students in the end had the same opinion of Shakespeare's *Othello* if they were all surreptitiously drilled in the same basic ideas? The problem of how to examine will always remain, especially in a national examination where large numbers of examiners have to be seen to be marking in the same way. It can only be hoped that in practice, as well as in theory, new courses encourage a wider spread of ideas and issues.

There has been quite a lot of controversy over the use of the Assessment Objective, not least among teachers – many say that if you divide everything up into 'jigsaw puzzle' units teaching becomes a farce. As I've already said, the question of how to teach and how to examine is not a simple one, just as the question of how to study English can be difficult. Because the AS/A2 system is new and we're still finding out how it will actually 'work', more changes may follow, and you should visit the QCA website (*www.qca.org.uk*) if you're interested in keeping up with the latest on the course outlines and assessment.

Learning about different approaches

All these different approaches and ideas might seem a bit threatening at first. And, of course, nobody can be expected to be an expert in a new way of seeing a text overnight, in the way one might memorise a set of facts. Instead, Barbara Bleiman and Lucy Webster, of the English and Media Centre, suggest that learning to read in a new way is a constantly developing process. They outline six rough steps in the process:

1   You'll always begin with your own initial response to the text. This could be enthusiastic or interested or even negative: whichever it is, you should think about why you responded like that.

2   It's important to listen carefully to the responses of your friends and other people in your class or seminar group. Somebody else may have seen something that you missed, or may have a very different take on the text.

3   You should begin to take on board what Bleiman and Webster call 'soundbites' about the text: short ideas or suggestions – provided by the teacher or lecturer perhaps – that illuminate the text and its context. (If these aren't provided for you, you might come up with some initial ideas from looking at, say, a guide to the author or period, or a relevant critical book.)

4   The next step would be to read essays or reviews of the novel, poem or play by other critics. Just like you, these critics will have presuppositions and points of view that they may or may not reveal in their work. Their presuppositions will guide their response to the text and you can begin to ask what 'position' each critic is writing from.

5   Rather than reading a critic who develops her or his own presuppositions, you could yourself explore different critical positions on the text (you could think of yourself as a feminist critic, say, or one who is interested in the ethical or political issues in a text). Arguing from a certain position can be very revealing, and it also involves discovering something about the critical approaches themselves. (You will probably have begun to think about these approaches in step 4.)

6   The last step is when a critical position is one that you 'own', when a set of ideas becomes part of your 'literary critical' tool kit, always ready to hand.

And this, sixth stage, leads back, of course, to the first stage – only now your initial response will be much more informed and analytic. Indeed, another reason why there is no right answer is that there is no real end to this constantly developing process.

Perhaps these steps sound very mechanical and rather soul crushing. In fact, they are steps that we almost inevitably take in our reading and our enjoyment of texts. One way we deepen our enjoyment of books, poems and plays (and other things – music, machines, history, fashion) is to find out more about them and to listen to (and evaluate) the views of others. In literature we have the ideas and views on texts from lots of interesting people going back over years, and this should help us enjoy the experience of reading more. Sometimes we don't enjoy texts straight away, and the thoughts of other people can help us discover ways in which we can enjoy them. (For example, I found that I really didn't like the work of the novelist Henry James [1843–1916] when I had to study him. Later, I read a particular critic's view of his work. Although I didn't agree with her ideas, it made me think about James again. I explained to myself why I didn't agree with her. This – rather suddenly, wonderfully and pleasurably – opened up James's novels for me, as if I had been shown into a beautiful new room.) That is, sometimes we need to become 'attuned' to a work, and other ideas about it can really help with this. Of course, sometimes you just don't enjoy a book at all, but that too is fascinating. To ask why you don't like something is very revealing about it and about you, and an important part of doing English.

The future of English

I have written, in this chapter, as if these changes in how we 'do English' have already been made; in fact, though they have been introduced, they are still very controversial. Because the 'traditional' approach was so completely taken for granted, for so many years, many people can't see what's wrong with what they do 'naturally' and don't see a need for change. Interestingly, many people outside education and with other agendas feel that they have a stake in English and have strong feelings about 'how English should be done'. This, in addition to the importance of English as a subject (which I will discuss in Part IV), means that any disputes or changes in the subject quickly become public controversies. Moreover, many of the ideas of theory can seem quite threatening. This is because theory reveals that every way of reading, even the traditional one, has presuppositions and that these are sometimes questionable. This means that the people who espouse more traditional approaches, rather than just presupposing that they are right, now have to argue for their ideas like everybody else. Many people are also unhappy when faced with the idea that there could be, as theory seems to suggest, no one right, final answer. In this case, they would rather maintain the fiction that there is one correct interpretation. However, not everyone has the opportunity to take part in the important arguments. A small group of people put together the outlines and reading lists for any course, and decide how it will be examined. If those making the decisions are resistant to 'theory', the older way of doing English will be preserved. Of course, the opposite is also true: if those 'in power' are friendly towards newer approaches, they will be able to create a broader-based course. In the UK example, the QCA write the Assessment Objectives, which are then worked into course outlines by small numbers of examiners working for a Board, who in turn advise teachers and markers on the courses. One way of thinking about the situation is to say that the Assessment Objectives are a text like any other, interpreted variously by the examiners (who award the grades), depending upon their own contexts. Certainly, when the new AS and A2 courses were introduced, many teachers read through a variety of Boards' outlines in order to find the one which seemed to reflect their own positions most closely, and there is quite a range of interpretation.

Whatever the detail of how and why, the ideas stimulated by theory are filtering across to a wider range of courses than ever before. As Patrick Scott suggested, the continuing dominance of one way of interpreting, particularly at secondary level, was damaging to students and to the discipline of English. It eroded for many people all that is stimulating and beneficial about studying literature, leaving English dogmatic, self-contradictory and exclusive. It limited creativity in students and teachers and it disregarded interesting and important ideas about literature, and so about ourselves, others, our lives and our world. It may seem daunting having to 'start again' with new ideas and approaches, but understanding why you need to do so is a very good beginning. As this book develops, I hope that my discussion of key issues in English today will show you how exciting English can be, and will encourage you to take this leap.

Summary

- Many people argued that the traditional approach to literature must be the right one, as it seems to be 'natural'. In fact, it is as much a 'learned' technical system of reading as any other literary theory.
- Reading literature in the 'one right way' meant 'theme-hunting', agreeing with what others say rather than arguing about a text, reducing a complex work to one 'right' phrase, seeing subjectivity as a weakness and finding texts hard to read because they had to be read through one particular set of presuppositions.
- One way of resolving this is the introduction of clear Assessment Objectives, as has happened in the UK at AS/A2 level. These set out clearly what students have to do, encourage knowledge of

other approaches and stress that you need an awareness of both the historical and the current contexts of a text.

- Learning about these new approaches cannot happen overnight: it is a constantly developing process.
- English is still a very controversial subject. But learning about literary theory can lead to all sorts of exciting new ideas about English, literature and the world.

4

Critical attitudes

- Where should we start with thinking about how we read?
- What is the intrinsic attitude?
- What is the extrinsic attitude?

English can appear to be quite daunting once you realise that there's an infinite number of ways you can read. If you're told to explore different methods of interpretation, challenge your presuppositions and think about how you, where are you supposed to start?

In the last chapter, I suggested that learning about different critical approaches or theories is a *process* that you go through. A step in this process is to look for patterns in the way these critical approaches work. To do this is to look for the presuppositions behind them and to think about the contexts in which texts are understood. In this chapter I shall outline one pattern which can be used as a starting point for thinking about a wide variety of critical approaches.

Into the text or *out from the text*?

If you look at a painting, are you looking through a window to another world or are you simply looking at the composition of colour and shape on a flat canvas? If you see a painting as a *window*, you might be concerned with what is going on behind the window: who the people are, say, and why they had their picture painted. You might ask about the historical significance of, for example, the skull on the shelf or even why the painter chose that particular subject in the first place. If, however, a picture is only a flat canvas, then you would ask different questions: about how the tones contrast, or how the shapes relate to one another. You might just be struck by the beautiful range of colours.

This same contrast occurs in thinking about literature. When you read a novel, poem or play, how do you approach it? Do you look at it as a beautifully woven fabric of language? Or as an example of writing which tells you about the historical period in which it was written? Is it stimulating because it puts words together in a new way? Or because it pours out on paper the intense experiences and interesting ideas of a particular writer? When we do English, do we study literary works for their pure artistic merit or because they reveal things about the world and their authors? Do you think of yourself as going *into* the text for itself or coming *out from* the text to explore other issues?

One of the longest debates in English has been about whether interpretation should focus on the text as a text itself (a flat canvas) or on the text as evidence for something else, such as its historical period and its attitudes, or an author's life (a window on a world). In an influential book called *Theory of Literature*, published as long ago as 1949, two critics, René Wellek and Austin Warren, called these two contrasting positions the *intrinsic* and *extrinsic* approaches to literature. These two terms are not the names for critical approaches themselves – instead they name contrasting sorts of presuppositions, tendencies or *attitudes* taken by approaches to literary texts. This debate, because it discusses what happens when we interpret in different ways and compares different methods of interpretation, is an example of hermeneutics, the study of interpretation. Certainly the debate has become more complex since 1949, but it is a very good place to start.

Intrinsic attitudes: into the text

The intrinsic attitude is often called 'formalism' because it is concerned, above all else, with the *form* of the text, its structure and language. It assumes that there is something special and uniquely 'literary' in the way literary texts use language. Because of this, the intrinsic attitude concentrates on the language of the text as its central object, considering things like the choice of metaphors, the use of symbols, structure, style, contrasts, images, and the development of the plot, to work out what a text means. Although these forms of criticism might sound rather dull and unrewarding, following the intricate paths taken in a text and looking closely at the twists and turns of its language can produce quite remarkable readings and effects. In fact, the very intense scrutiny of the 'words on the page' can result in the most unusual and challenging interpretations of texts, as the multiple and often unclear meanings of each word are weighed up and evaluated. As you concentrate on the words themselves, their meaning becomes not clearer, but more ambiguous (or *indeterminate*). This is most obvious when looking at poetry.

For example, there is a sonnet by the English poet William Wordsworth (1770–1850) called 'Composed upon Westminster Bridge', which describes all of London, seen from the bridge at dawn, stretched out and radiant: 'Earth has not anything to show more fair' and the city 'like a garment' wears 'the beauty of the morning'. The poem finishes with these lines:

> Dear God! The very houses seem asleep
> And all that mighty heart is lying still.

The first meaning of 'lying still' is that the city is spread out, not moving, lying motionless asleep. But the word 'lying' has another meaning, of course: to lie is not to tell the truth. Perhaps the sonnet is implying that the city, *despite* all the beauty of the morning light, is *still* not telling the truth. The sunrise makes London look wonderful but really the city, 'that mighty heart', is still a den of deceit, corruption, falsehood and lies. By concentrating on the language – on the *form* of the text – two separate readings have emerged. On the one hand, London is beautiful, quiet and still in the dawn light. On the other, London *seems* beautiful, but underneath and despite all this beauty it is deceitful and corrupt. These readings are contradictory and mutually exclusive: either London is really deeply beautiful and peaceful or it's actively scheming, lying and dishonest. Which reading you choose depends on the way you interpret 'lying still'.

All ways of reading share this concentration on language to some extent, but, for the critics who tend towards the intrinsic attitude, doing English is principally a matter of looking at the words on the page with great rigour. This sort of criticism first characterised the subject of English in the 1920s and 1930s. It was first most fully outlined in I. A. Richards' book *Practical Criticism* (1929). Richards gave poems out to his students, without the poets' names, dates, or any other information that might give the students ideas about the texts outside 'the words on the page'. He asked for their responses ('practical criticism') and collected the results. He felt that this was a useful way to study what he considered to be special about literature – its 'literary-ness'. For Richards, and those he inspired, 'literary-ness' is the special sort of manipulation of language that happens, they argue, only in literature, and this is where its value, and possibly its 'moral worth', lies. This idea spread to the USA in the 1930s and 1940s and became a key pre-supposition of the approach to literature known as 'New Criticism'. The methods of interpretation that take this intrinsic approach for granted are often still called 'practical criticism' or 'close reading'.

This sort of intrinsic approach to literature is still very influential and important (in fact, some form of 'close reading' of texts is central to most subjects). When you are asked to do a 'practical criticism', 'write an appreciation' or 'appraisal', 'analyse the main poetic methods', pay 'close attention to meaning, language and structure', investigate the 'style' or 'narrative technique', or even 'comment on the author's skill in suggesting unspoken feelings through incident and description', you are being asked to take an intrinsic approach to literature. Even questions on character or plot, although they seem to have a wider focus, usually lead you to take this approach. Think about how you'd read a text in order to answer the following questions (typical of the 'old' A level):

- How far do you see the relationship between Hamlet and Claudius as the central conflict of the play?
- What is the function of the minor characters in the novel?
- Describe a dramatic scene from the novel and discuss its importance to the novel as a whole.

You wouldn't need any knowledge outside of the play or the novel to be able to answer the questions.

Although it might offer some interesting insights, used alone this intrinsic attitude does have blind spots and rests upon some rather large assumptions, as I outlined in Chapter 2. To recap: some critics claim that intrinsic types of criticism lead to 'objective' readings, the idea that texts can be independent of their historical, social and personal context, and that 'literary-ness' makes a text a valuable work of art, which is worth studying in its own right. However, even if you claim only to be looking at the text by itself you bring your own ideas, expectations and experiences to it. How can any judgement of worth be objective?

Extrinsic attitudes: out of the text

In contrast, extrinsic methods of interpretation take it for granted that the literary text is part of the world and rooted in its context. An extrinsic critic considers that the job of criticism is to move from the text outwards to some other, not specifically literary, object or idea. Such critics use literary texts to explore other ideas about things in the world, and in turn use other ideas to explain the literary text.

Perhaps the most important and widespread sort of extrinsic criticism is the way of reading that puts texts firmly into their historical context. This is why the extrinsic attitude is often referred to as *historicist*. Historicist criticism, and there are many versions of it, uses literary texts to explore or discuss historical issues, and conversely it uses history and context to explain literary texts. In dealing with Shakespeare's *King Lear*, for example, a historicist critic might look through the play to find clues about what was expected of a king at the time Shakespeare was writing, and how the ruler and the nation were thought to be woven together. By the same token, a historicist critic might also use evidence from Shakespeare's time and its historical context to explain the play. But historicist criticism is not limited to works from the past: you could use another form of historical criticism to study a contemporary popular novel – a 'bestseller'. Looking at the way people behave in the novel, even if it might not be considered a great work of art, would reveal all sorts of interesting contemporary social attitudes. If the leading female character, for example, is constantly and obsessively counting the calories she consumes, units of alcohol she drinks and number of cigarettes she smokes, this might indicate, for example, how strongly women in contemporary Western society feel forced to live up to an 'ideal' model of body-shape and behaviour.

Many of the newer ways of reading are based on the extrinsic attitude. Critics who use psychoanalysis as a way of reading might understand a literary text as a product of the author's psychology, or as a way of understanding parts of the human mind in general. In fact, the work of Sigmund Freud (1856–1939) and other psychoanalysts has been widely used to interpret literary works. Those who explicitly champion political positions use literary texts as evidence for wider historical and political arguments. The many forms of feminist criticism use literary texts to explore the roles of women and men, amongst other things. Other critics start with the text and draw conclusions about, say, nature, humanity or the pitfalls of love. Even approaches that consider the author's intention or her or his life display the extrinsic attitude, since neither the author nor her or his biography are actually *in* the text.

The idea of looking beyond a text to 'the world' is very attractive to those who emphasise the way in which literature is linked to the world. Many new forms of extrinsic criticism have emerged in the last twenty years or so as academics have sought ways of reflecting the changes in contemporary society. The emphasis on new literary theories at university means that you spend a lot of time learning about extrinsic approaches. The new assessement objectives for AS and A2, by mentioning contexts and different readers' interpretations, have also begun to move towards extrinsic approaches. Those who oppose extrinsic critical attitudes point to the fact that in using this approach you start with a literary text, but move away to an object or idea that is *not specifically literary*. They argue that in doing so you do not actually deal with literature itself at all, but rather with politics, the mind, history, gender relations, biography and so on. If you approach a text as if it were a piece of evidence for history, opponents say, then it is no different from a treaty, a will, or any other piece of historical documentation. If you read a novel to learn about the author, the novel itself is no more than a piece of evidence for a biography and no different from a diary entry. What makes the text special as 'literature' is not of interest.

Contrasting these two attitudes

Looking at the key aspects of these attitudes, as shown in Table 4.1, is a useful way to compare and contrast them.

Table 4.1 Intrinsic and extrinsic critical attitudes

Intrinsic attitude	Extrinsic attitude
Into the text	Out from the text to the context
A flat canvas	A window
Literature is worth studying in its own right: it uses language in a unique way	Literature is worth studying for what it tells us about other things
'Great texts' are the focus because they have artistic and possibly moral worth	Any sort of text is worthy of study, as they all reveal 'the world'
'Formalism'	'Historicism'
'Words on the page'	Context
Meanings often indeterminate	Context decides meaning
Practical criticism, 'close reading' and New Criticism	Historicism; psychoanalytical criticism; explicitly political criticism; feminisms; philosophical criticism; biography and other sorts of criticism
Text stands alone	Text only has meaning in context
Knowledge of the text alone	Knowledge of the context (history, author's life and so on)
Style, plot, character	Theme, setting

These oppositions have been the subject of fierce debate and you will come across signs of this at different levels and in different ways right through the discipline of English. Both these general attitudes are valid, as are the critical methods they stimulate. Even if they do have 'blind spots', both have a role to play in English as a whole. Sometimes the most useful works of criticism are produced by a coming-together of these two attitudes in different ways.

Thinking about these general patterns helps to orient you by explaining why approaches to literature have developed in the way they have. This introductory guide to critical attitudes also makes it more straightforward for you to draw parallels between different approaches and to explore the presuppositions and blind spots of any particular approach.

Summary

- One way to think about the presupposition of reading is to divide critical theories into two broad groups or attitudes: intrinsic and extrinsic.
- Intrinsic ways of reading concentrate on *words on the page*. A work is considered separate from the world and the focus is on its internal features. Critics who support the intrinsic attitude rely on language and structure to decide what a text means.
- Extrinsic ways of reading look beyond the text *to the context*. The literary text is seen as part of the world and critics move through the words on the page to broader, non-literary ideas, like history or biography, which are in turn used to explain what a text might mean.
- Both these attitudes have blind spots and gaps. Intrinsic approaches are criticised for assuming that there can be an objective way of reading and for separating literature from 'the real world'. Extrinsic attitudes are criticised for failing to see 'literature' as something special and preferring to discuss non-literary ideas.
- Thinking about these general patterns helps to orient you when you look at different critical approaches, helps you to draw parallels between different approaches and to explore the presuppositions of any particular approach.

PART II

WHAT WE READ

5

Literature, value and the canon

- Can literature be defined?
- What is literary value?
- What is the canon?
- How does the canon affect you?

If, as I have argued, we need to think about how we read, we also need to think about what we read. Debates over the texts you should read, and even what literature is, have become very important to English studies.

Can literature be defined?

When we go into a bookshop or library, we know basically what to expect in the literature section. But if we try to answer the question 'What is literature?', no definition seems satisfactory. There are always countless exceptions to every rule. For example, if you defined literature as *fiction*, where would you put fact-based writing, such as autobiographies, or plays and novels that portray historical events? Where would you put the poems that claim not to be fictional but to reveal a 'higher' truth? If you wanted to suggest that literature '*represents the world*' (that it was, to use the technical term, *mimetic*), what would you do with the surreal poems, plays and novels, which don't seem to represent the world at all? And, after all, don't other forms of writing – historical, scientific – claim to represent the world as well? Literature can't exclusively be something that '*tells a story*', either. How would this be any different from, for example, a medical textbook 'telling the story' of the symptoms caused by a particular disease or a scientist detailing what happens in an experiment to measure cosmic rays?

You might argue that a work of literature was something that *moved* you or *entertained* you, but what would you call a novel that moved one of your friends but left you cold? You might call it 'bad literature', but would you say it wasn't literature at all? Again, if you wanted to argue that literature should convey a message, what would you do with writing that didn't seem to convey messages, or literature that was utterly unclear about exactly what message it might be carrying? Besides any of this, couldn't you argue that a song or a sandwich might move you just as much as words on paper?

It is easier to understand literature not as something that can be defined, but as something that *overflows* or *escapes* from any attempt to limit it or put it in a box. As you try to give it a definite meaning, literature slips through your fingers like water. But then, perhaps literature is not a 'thing' at all, which is why it slips away when you try to categorise it. Reading, after all, is more like a process you are engaged in, something you do. Perhaps literature is more like a verb, a 'doing', than it is a noun or thing.

All this is made more complex by the fact that, historically, the category of texts known as 'literature' has changed a great deal. In fact, as Rob Pope argues in *The English Studies Book*, when the word was first used in the English language, from the late fourteenth century, it didn't mean a type of text at all, but rather what we now call 'literacy', a sort of 'knowledge of books'. In the nineteenth century, 'literature' did mean a body of writing, but included what we would call history, biography, philosophy, sociology, science and much more. It simply meant something written on a certain subject. We still have this sense of literature – a pile of pamphlets about technological advances might be called 'scientific literature' – but somehow we have invented a separate category called Literature, with a capital L, which means something quite different.

The philosophical and historical discussions over the identity of literature lead to a fundamental question for anyone studying English: if there is no clear, defined area of study, how do you decide which texts to read?

After all, there are too many books to read in any one lifetime. When we do English, we *choose* our literary texts or, more accurately, *the texts are chosen for us*. Those who have made the choices and shaped the English syllabus have done so with a certain idea in mind: that of literary value.

What is literary value?

Often when we say literature, we say it with a capital L, Literature. Knowingly or not, the term is used to make a *value judgement* about the *worth* of a piece of writing. People say 'this is a truly great novel, it's Literature' or they say 'that's only a thriller (or horror story or romance), it's not proper Literature'. In this sense, Literature doesn't just mean words on pages, but a certain sort of highly valued and important writing. It used to be taken for granted that people studying literature read only 'great' literature – or Literature. There are even lists of 'great books' we should read and admire, known as 'the canon'. This is why the same novels, poems and plays turn up again and again on literature courses and in exams. In no small way, doing English means reading, studying and writing about the canon. It affects your courses, exams, results and everything else about doing English. The content of the canon and the criteria for selection are among the most contentious issues in English – but what is the canon?

What is the canon?

The origins of the canon

Where the idea of the canon came from is unclear: the term itself comes from the Christian Church. Faced with a number of texts about Jesus and the early Christians and with the Hebrew Scriptures, and also with disputes about which sources to trust, the Catholic Church decided at the Council of Trent in 1546 that some of the texts were true sources of 'divine revelation' – and so were 'canonical' – and that others were not. The aim was to create a list of religious texts that everybody would accept as authentic and authoritative. Eighteenth-century philologists took this desire for 'authentic and authoritative' texts into the study of language. Because there were a huge number of forgeries of ancient Greek and Roman texts, these philologists aimed to establish a 'canon' of texts that were really Greek and Roman.

The poets and writers of the Renaissance (roughly 1450–1650) also produced lists, ranking the most important types, or *genres*, of writing ('genre' means 'kind' or 'type' of literary text). These days we have many genres of literary text, normally divided not by form but by content. In any bookshop there are shelves for all sorts of novel genres: thrillers, romances, science fiction, fantasy. These definitions can be even more detailed: a genre of novels set in universities (the 'campus novel'), thrillers where the lead character is a forensic scientist, perhaps. Many types of novel are often dismissed as simply 'genre fiction' and are almost always excluded from the traditional canon, although there is no reason to suppose that a science fiction novel, for example, would not be as interesting or rewarding to read as a 'literary' novel. Each genre has its own generic conventions, parts of plot or style that are special to that genre. These occur both in the content (you expect a murder in a whodunit, or a marriage at the end of a comic play) and in the style (for example, a spare, terse style in a hard-boiled detective story). Occasionally, texts mix up or blur these conventions for effect. In the Renaissance, however, these boundaries and definitions, so important to us today, were just beginning to take shape. In his book *Kinds of Literature*, Alastair Fowler shows how the British poet Sir Phillip Sidney (1554–1586) produced a list that classed poetry by type: epic, lyric, comic, satiric, elegiac, amatory, pastoral sonnet, epigram. Epic poetry was the greatest, most enduring and most significant form, while short poems about love were the most transient and insubstantial. By the eighteenth century it was common to find debates not only over the worth of particular genres of poetry, but also over the worth of particular writers. A critic called Joseph Warton (1722–1800) wrote that in 'the first class I would place our only three sublime and pathetic poets: Spenser, Shakespeare, Milton' ('pathetic' meant 'moving' or 'poignant' at this time). Such a reference to 'our' poets shows how the idea of literary value was becoming linked to that of nationalism.

The ideas of authority, authenticity, value and nationalism began to come together even more closely in the nineteenth century. Perhaps most influential in the formation of the canon were the many anthologies of poetry popular in the nineteenth century. The most famous of these was the *Golden Treasury of English Verse*, compiled by Francis Turner Palgrave (1824–1897), first published in 1861, often re-edited and republished. It's still in print and still popular today. The title of the *Golden Treasury of English Verse* is itself very revealing: just as the national treasury has the authority to make financial decisions on behalf of the nation, so a treasury of poetry has taken upon itself the authority to decide which poems should be considered the most valuable by its readers. Just as a nation's treasury contains the material goods – money – most valuable to its people, this treasury contains the poems most valuable to its readers. On the very first page, Palgrave said that he aimed to 'include ... all the best original Lyrical pieces and songs in our language, by writers not living – and none but the best'. In judging what to include or exclude, Palgrave used two criteria: the types (genres) of poetry and the 'genius' of the poet. No didactic poems (poems intended to instruct), no humorous poems and no narrative poems (those simply telling a story) were allowed in. Only poems relying on what he called 'some single thought, feeling or situation' were worthy to be allowed into the *Golden Treasury*. But the poems also had to be 'worthy of the writer's genius'. This means that the writer already had to be recognised as a major poet to be included, and the poem had to show off their particular talent. However, is it possible to be, as Palgrave claims he is, without 'caprice or particularity' about a writer's talent? In the 1861 edition of the *Golden Treasury*, for example, there were no poems by the radical working-class poet William Blake (1757–1827). Even more significantly, there were no poems by women in the early editions of the anthology. Does this show that a poet had to be of a certain class and gender before Palgrave would even consider their poems?

T. S. Eliot, the Leavises and the canon

These historical threads form the backdrop to the development of the modern canon. What we recognise as the canon today grew up hand in hand with the discipline of English in the 1920s. It is here that the assumptions of value, authenticity and authority come clearly into focus and become ever more closely linked with nationalism. As mentioned in Chapter 1, major figures in this development were the poet and critic T. S. Eliot (1888–1965) and the critics F. R. Leavis (1895–1978) and Q. D. Leavis (1906–1981).

Although T. S. Eliot is now thought of principally as a poet, his essays of literary criticism in the 1920s were extremely influential; indeed, E. M. W. Tillyard, a critic of the time, described them as 'revolutionary'. One of his most important essays was 'Tradition and the Individual

Talent', published in two parts in 1919, in which Eliot argues that each artist writes in relation to a tradition,

> not merely with his own generation in his bones, but with a feeling that the whole of the literature of Europe from Homer and within it the whole of the literature of his own country has a simultaneous existence and composes a simultaneous order.

For Eliot, a tradition isn't just the past but a living thing, organised, structured and present in the mind – or even in the bones – of a great writer (always a 'he' for Eliot). This 'living tradition' of great literature makes up what Eliot later calls an 'ideal order', which ranks the great and valuable works. This is clearly a canon. In order to write a great poem, novel or play, or to appreciate a great work of literary art fully, Eliot argues that it is necessary that 'we' have these works in their 'ideal order' in our 'bones'. If this order is in our bones, it is part of who we are, not something we have to think about. 'We' must have internalised and accepted not only the list of works that people like Palgrave decided were great but, more importantly, the criteria that guided their judgement.

Eliot's idea has two consequences. The first concerns what these authoritative texts are authoritatively telling you. An authoritative list of Classical texts tells you that certain texts are authentically ancient Greek or Roman and not forgeries or inventions; the authority of books of scripture lies in the fact that they are thought to reveal the authentic word of God. But what authenticity does an authoritative list of works of literature reveal? For Eliot and those influenced by him, what underlies a great literary work, what a great work reveals and so therefore what makes it 'authentic' are the values of Western European (and within that English) culture and life. The canon, he argues, is the 'storehouse of Western values'. These Western European values are unquestioningly assumed to be *universal human values*, the most important values that apply to all people at all times and in all places.

This leads to the second consequence: if a text doesn't seem to demonstrate these 'universal' values or expresses different ones, it is not considered valuable, and so is excluded from the canon. Eliot's seemingly innocent metaphor of 'bones' in fact reveals a rather frightening idea. It is as if it is not enough just to study the tradition – it must be in your bones, in your body. If you don't 'genetically' share the idea of the canon

and the 'universal' Western European values underlying it, you can neither properly appreciate nor write great books. In their book *The
Decolonization of African Literature*, Chinweizu, Onwuchekwa Jemie
and Ihechukwu Madubuike, a trio of African writers and critics, sum this
up from their perspective:

> most of the objections to . . . the African novel sound like admon-
> itions from imperialist mother hens to their wayward or outright
> rebellious captive chickens. They cluck: 'Be Universal! Be Uni-
> versal!' And what they don't consider universal they denounce as
> anthropological, atavistic [i.e. reverting to an earlier, primitive
> state], autobiographical, sociological, journalistic, topical ephem-
> era, as not literary.

Again, what doesn't reveal Western values (masquerading as universal
values) simply isn't authentic literature, is not worth reading and couldn't
be part of the canon.

The idea was further developed by F. R. Leavis. Following Eliot's lead,
he drew up a list of 'great writers'. Then, rather than saying that these
were his 'favourites', he asserted that they were quite simply the best. For
example, he begins his very influential work of 1948, *The Great Tradition*,
by stating that the 'great English Novelists are Jane Austen, George Eliot,
Henry James and Joseph Conrad'. Although he admits that other
novelists have merits, the best – the ones who most authentically reveal
the values he cherishes – are these four at the heart of the canon. The
reasons he chooses these four are hard to pin down exactly. He writes that
'they are significant in terms of that human awareness they promote:
awareness of the possibilities of life', and that they are 'creative geniuses
whose distinction is manifested in their being alive in their time'. This
manages to sound both convincing and authoritative and also rather
vague. Of course, it is interesting to find out which books acute and
well-read critics like the Leavises think are good. But their stamp of
authority establishes this not just as *a* list, but as *the* list we should all
share. As discussed earlier, they rely upon a personal sensibility to make
judgements they claim to be objective, again because they assume that
everyone shares or should share the same English and European values.
One of the reasons the Leavises fostered the study of English was to
cultivate a sense of national community, and it is clear that it also lay
behind the choice of books in their canon.

How does the canon affect you?

The canon today

The canon is still with us today. It is deeply woven into the fabric not just of English as a subject but into all forms of culture. TV and film adaptations tend to be of 'canonical' novels; publishers print 'classics'; to count as educated you are supposed to have read a smattering of 'canonical novels'. Why is the canon such a powerful idea?

First, the canon is a reflection that English always has a social *context* and could never be done in a vacuum. The canon represents the meeting point between (1) judgements of the artistic (or *aesthetic*) value of a text, and (2) the presupposition and interests, either implicit or explicit, of those who make those judgements and have the power to enforce them. What makes the issue difficult is that, despite claims to be 'objective' or 'neutral', it is very, very hard to separate out an artistic or aesthetic judgement from a judgement based on position and interests. These two are interwoven.

Second, the canon is *self-perpetuating*. In English at all levels, the same canonical texts come up again and again, year after year. A person who studied English and has become a teacher often teaches the texts she or he was taught, in part because she or he was taught that these texts were the most important. As students, you expect to study texts you have heard of and assume are worthwhile and, of course, resources that support your study, such as websites, IT resources, guidebooks or videos of productions, concentrate on canonical texts, which in a way makes them easier to study. (After all, why would a company produce a guidebook to a novel that only a few people have heard of?) Many textbooks for English and books on literature in general assume a familiarity with the canon, which also underlines its centrality. In fact, textbooks from earlier in the twentieth century were often made up literally of lists and descriptions of great books. A more recent version of this is *The Western Canon* from 1994, by the American critic Harold Bloom. This book is a long defence of the idea of the canon, and ends with a list of the thousand books (he thinks) everyone 'cultured' should have read. The canon, then, is the list of books you expect to study when you do English, and reading the canon is doing English. The subject and the canon in part define each other.

However, even those who make and publish actual lists of 'great books' admit that sometimes the lists can change, as certain books come into and out of favour. But the third reason the canon is so powerful is that it *creates the criteria by which texts are judged.* It sounds like common sense to say that the texts you study must be of 'high quality' and worthy of 'serious consideration', but these sort of statements give no sort of yardstick to measure this; the values that make a work substantial and give it 'quality' are not revealed. New or rediscovered texts are judged by the canon's standards. This means that even when, for example, AS and A2 exam boards choose books from a wider selection of texts than normal, they will probably first ask if the books have 'universal significance', 'positive values' or 'human significance'. Saying that a new novel fits the canon because it 'has' these, reaffirms the idea that an older novel 'had' them too. Paradoxically, the canon is not broken up, but reaffirmed.

The fourth reason the canon remains powerful is that it is involved with the senses of *identity* to which countries and groups aspire, and with the struggle to define identities. As the history of the canon suggested, its development was tied in with the development of ideas about nationality. It is for this reason that Toni Morrison (b. 1931), the Nobel prize-winning American author, wrote in 1989 that

> Canon building is empire building. Canon defence is national defence. Canon debate, whatever the terrain, nature and range (of criticism, of history, of the history of knowledge, of the definition of language, the universality of aesthetic principles, the sociology of art, the humanist imagination) is the clash of cultures. And *all* the interests are vested.

Because it is canonical texts that are taught, studied, examined, published, sold, bought, performed, made into TV mini-series, adapted for YouTube parodies updated into contemporary settings in films and for bestsellers and so on, the canon plays a significant role in creating a sense of shared culture and of collective national identity. Deciding which texts are in the canon is all part of deciding who we are and how we want to see ourselves, and a threat to the canon is a threat to national identity. But does the person creating your course ask how you want to see yourself? As Toni Morrison says, all the interests are vested.

Canons tomorrow?

Because there are simply too many books to read within the limits of any course, decisions have to be made. However, since the canon and the texts you study are so important, these decisions stimulate furious debate. Brian Cox (1928–2008), a key figure in the development of the discipline of English from the 1960s to the present day, believes that 'our ideas of the canon constantly change, and lists of great books should never be inscribed in a parliamentary order, and so inscribed in stone'. He was outraged when he discovered that, after curriculum revisions in 1992, 'it soon became apparent that the lists of set authors would include very few non-British writers, with an occasional name such as Derek Walcott thrown in as a token gesture'. (Walcott is a Nobel prize-winning poet and playwright. He was born in St Lucia in the Caribbean in 1930 and writes in English.) The debates over the canon and course specifications will go on. But, slowly, the canon is breaking down, as new approaches and new ideas affect which books people decide to teach and study.

Indeed, English at secondary level and in higher education is playing a role in changing the canon in the UK. The QCA demand that more living writers and a wider range of genres are to be studied has already changed what is thought of as 'canonical'.

Nevertheless, the *idea* of the canon is still very powerful. If the single monolithic canon is breaking down, an array of separate canons has taken its place. There are canons of African-American writing, of women's writing, and of science fiction, for example. Texts that were previously marginalised by 'the canon' now are considered important and have canons of their own. Those doing English have more freedom to choose one canon over another.

The power of the canon makes it essential for us to question what we read. How did it get into the canon? Why? What were the values of those who chose the text? As part of this process of questioning the canon, I will now turn to the figure at the centre of the canon, and (some might argue) at the centre of the discipline of English itself: William Shakespeare.

Summary

- No definitions of 'literature' seem to be adequate: literature overflows or escapes from any attempt to categorise it.
- Often unknowingly, we make value judgements about writing:

literature comes to mean a certain sort of highly valued and important writing.

- The list of 'great books' that we should read and admire is known as 'the canon'. The process by which texts are chosen to be part of the canon depends upon (questionable) ideas of authenticity, authority, nationalism and literary value.

- The canon is still with us today, woven into the fabric of Western culture. It is the meeting point between artistic judgement and wider presuppositions; it is self-perpetuating; it sets up the criteria by which texts are judged; it is involved with our sense of identity.

- The canon appears to be changing, and developing into 'canons'. However it is still vital to know how and why any canon is constructed.

6

Doing Shakespeare

- Why is Shakespeare so central to studying English literature?
- What are the traditional arguments for studying Shakespeare?
- What are some of the new ideas about studying Shakespeare?
- How do these ideas affect the way we study Shakespeare?

Chapter 5 examined the canon in general, and this chapter is going to examine debates about the texts that have been assumed to be the very centre of the canon – the plays of William Shakespeare (1564–1616). Debate rages over approaches to Shakespeare, but this discussion is rarely explained to students.

Castle Shakespeare

Shakespeare has become a literary institution, seen by many teachers and lecturers as the unquestionable centre of English studies, and a figure familiar to anyone who knows anything about literature. In her book *Letters to Alice, on First Reading Jane Austen*, the contemporary novelist Fay Weldon (b. 1933) suggests that writers 'build Houses of Imagination' in 'the City of Invention'. This city has an 'all male suburb of sci-fi', a 'Romance alley' and 'public buildings and worthy monuments, which some find boring and others magnificent'. The city is a particularly interesting metaphor for literary value, since, just as in any city, some districts are 'better' than others. She writes that at the 'heart of the city is the great Castle Shakespeare. You see it whichever way you look. It rears its head into the clouds reaching into the celestial sky, dominating everything around.' Although the huge castle is a 'rather uneven building, frankly . . . shoddy, and rather carelessly constructed in parts', Weldon writes that it 'keeps standing through the centuries and, build as others may, they can never quite achieve the same grandeur; and the visitors keep flocking, and the guides keep training and re-training, finding yet new ways of explaining the old building'. Weldon is showing us the way Shakespeare holds his place at the heart of the canon, while, apparently, other authors try in vain to achieve his stature and literary critics offer new ways of approaching his work.

But the institution of Shakespeare stretches well beyond the world of literature. Jonathan Bate, a leading Shakespearean specialist, writes in his book *The Genius of Shakespeare*:

> In British life he seems to be everywhere. He is quoted and adapted daily in newspaper headlines and advertising copy . . . He has a national, massively subsidised theatre company named after him and committed to the regular revival of all his works. Driving down the M6 motorway, you pass signs indicating the new county you are entering: Cheshire, Staffordshire, Warwickshire. But the sign does not say Warwickshire – it says 'Warwickshire: Shakespeare's County'. Handing over a cheque guarantee card, one presents as a mark of its authenticity a hologram of Shakespeare's head.

On 1 January 1999, listeners to BBC Radio 4's news and current-affairs programme *Today* voted Shakespeare the 'British Person of the Millennium'. Shakespeare's phrases have even entered the English language. As the journalist Bernard Levin pointed out, if you have ever not slept a wink, refused to budge an inch, made a virtue of necessity, knitted your brows, stood on ceremony, had short shrift, cold comfort or too much of a good thing, you're quoting Shakespeare. The philosopher Ludwig Wittgenstein (1889–1951) called him 'an inventor of language'.

Shakespeare is considered so important by so many people in the United Kingdom that he is the only compulsory author on the National

Curriculum and the only author named by the Qualifications and Curriculum Authority in their guidelines. This means that it is effectively a legal requirement for anybody educated in the UK to study Shakespeare. After women's writing, his work is the most studied subject on university English syllabuses – which makes him by far the most-studied single author.

However, it's not immediately obvious to everyone why you should have to study Shakespeare, and certainly not to students. For an article called 'Reading Shakespeare, or Ways with Will', John Yandell, Head of English at an East London school, asked a group of 12- and 13-year-olds why they would be studying Shakespeare in the year ahead. They gave various answers: 'It's part of our education'; 'Because he was the best'; 'You don't hear of no other people who do plays like him'; 'When his plays came out, the first people who saw it thought it was really good, but it's hard for us to understand it because times have changed'; 'We've got to because of the exam; because the play is written in English'.

These different answers are all, in fact, quite similar. To say that you have to study Shakespeare's plays for the exam, or because they are on the curriculum, or simply because they're in English, is only to say, really, that you study Shakespeare's plays 'because you're told to'. The students who say, before they've actually studied Shakespeare, that he is the best or that the first people who saw his plays thought them excellent also sound as if really they're answering 'because we're told to': they have been *told* that the plays are the best or were much appreciated by early audiences, so they have taken Shakespeare's excellence for granted. John Yandell interviewed teachers, too. One responded,

> when kids go 'I hate Shakespeare' I can honestly say 'I really understand that, I'm not telling you that it's brilliant'. And sometimes they ask 'Why have we got to study this?' and the personal side of me thinks 'I haven't got an answer for that – I had to, you have to' . . . it's never very satisfactory.

Several other teachers felt the same – 'I had to, you have to'.

The same question arises: But why? There must be better reasons to study Shakespeare than 'because you have to'. Certainly many critics and academics have tried to offer reasons. As with many other issues in English, the study of Shakespeare is the focus of a highly contentious debate, which has not yet filtered down to most students. This debate has been running since the mid-1970s, when all that was 'traditional English' began to come into question. As Shakespeare was (and still is) seen by so many as central to English courses, the debate over why he should be studied has led to some particularly fierce arguments. Roughly speaking, there are two camps: on the one hand there are those who might be called the *traditionalists*; on the other are a number of critics whom Jonathan Bate describes as the 'New Iconoclasts' (an 'iconoclast' is literally an 'icon-breaker', and means a person who attacks established ideas). Many of those who attack the institution of Shakespeare describe themselves as *cultural materialists*. As you might expect, there is no neutral view on this: both camps have presuppositions that determine their opinions. The rest of this chapter sketches their arguments, then outlines what effect these have for doing English.

Studying Shakespeare: the traditionalists' argument

Shakespeare's friend Ben Jonson (1572–1637) wrote that Shakespeare is 'not of an age, but for all time': this might be the motto of the traditionalists' argument for the study of Shakespeare. Simply, they argue or assume that Shakespeare's plays are the greatest literary texts, which makes the study of them invaluable. It is possible to break this argument down into three parts:

- the artistic (or aesthetic) worth of Shakespeare's plays
- the values taught by Shakespeare's plays
- the universal appeal of Shakespeare's work.

The traditionalists' argument suggests that Shakespeare's plays are unarguably the pinnacle of literary art and that their aesthetic worth cannot be rivalled. There are examples of this unquestioned assumption all over the place. *Desert Island Discs*, a long-running radio programme, again on BBC Radio 4, hypothetically leaves its guests stranded on an abandoned island with eight records of their choice, a luxury item, the Bible, a book of their choice and – because it's the best – the *Complete Works of Shakespeare*. You may come across a student guide called *Studying Shakespeare*, by Katherine Armstrong and Graham Arkin. This asks 'Why study Shakespeare?', then answers by saying 'We need look no further than the opening exchange of *Hamlet*.' The authors offer a critical analysis of the passage and repeat the process with passages from the plays *As You Like It* and *King Lear*. This is as if to say, 'If we just look at a passage of Shakespeare, its brilliance will convince us that Shakespeare is the best and so deserves more study than the work of other writers.' Academic and journalist James Wood discussed the end of *King Lear* in a review: 'it is difficult to watch King Lear and not hear people crying at this moment in the play'. Shakespeare here is simply seen as the most moving, as the greatest, of all writers.

Traditionalists also argue that Shakespeare is the best teacher of values. Sometimes this is in the form of windy rhetoric: exaggerated praise and empty words. In his book *Representative Men* (1850), American poet and critic Ralph Waldo Emerson (1803–1882) wrote of Shakespeare:

> What point of morals, of manners, of economy, of philosophy, of religion, of taste, of the conduct of life, has he not settled? What mystery has he not signified his knowledge of? What office, or function, or district of man's work, has he not remembered? What king has he not taught state . . . ? What maiden has not found him finer than her delicacy? What lover has he not outloved? What sage has he not outseen? What gentleman has he not instructed in the rudeness of his behavior?

Shakespeare is seen as a font of wisdom and a source of truth about human behaviour, good and bad. For traditionalists, literature teaches values and ideals and Shakespeare's works are the highest form of literature. This means that to study Shakespeare is not just to study one man's work but to study 'the human spirit' at its finest.

What is particularly interesting is that people with very different values find their own values reflected in Shakespeare. For example, in his book *Shakespeare*, the critic Kiernan Ryan describes how the plays 'sharpen our need to forge a world from which division has been purged'. For him, Shakespeare's plays are radical, suggesting that the established order needs to be shaken up and reformed. In contrast, as Jonathan Bate points out, the former right-wing British politician Michael Portillo quoted Shakespeare's play *Troilus and Cressida* in a speech in 1994 to explain 'how order in society depends on a series of relationships of respect and duty from top to bottom'. He was attacking those who 'had become "cynical" about Britain's ancient institutions and traditional values' and so defending the established order and its divisions from high to low.

Both these examples focus on the 'universal' values the plays are said to present.

This leads to the final part of the traditionalists' views: that because everybody is moved and affected by Shakespeare's plays, Shakespeare embodies universal values and has something to say to all people at all times and in all places. Traditionalists often suggest that anybody seeing or reading the plays feels that Shakespeare is speaking to them and their innermost thoughts. In a lecture in 1990, the American poet, writer and activist Maya Angelou (b. 1928) described her love for Shakespeare. Growing up in poverty in the southern United States and experiencing American racism, she said that she felt Shakespeare spoke to her so completely that she knew 'William Shakespeare was a black woman'. The traditionalists argue that Shakespeare's works should be studied precisely because of this universal quality. They might be said to express the basic emotions, thoughts, ideas, hopes and fears of everybody in the world.

For the traditionalists, Shakespeare's plays are like a star: beautiful, remote, independent of the earth and worldly concerns, to be wondered at and admired. Yet, like medieval sailors navigating by the night sky, we are given direction by the star. It gives us core values, and by studying Shakespeare we learn those values.

Using Shakespeare: the cultural materialists' argument

Opposed to the traditionalist arguments are critics and thinkers who can roughly be described as *cultural materialists*. A cultural-materialist critic is principally interested in the way material factors – like economic conditions and political struggles of all sorts – have influenced or even created a text. In turn, they argue that any text can tell us about these material conditions. Because their interest is in the context of works, they argue that all works of culture – here, Shakespeare's plays – are involved with politics and the world. (This reveals the extrinsic attitude I discussed in Chapter 4, where critics look beyond the text to other non-literary ideas.) For a cultural materialist, 'Shakespeare' – both the plays and the institution – is a construct of present-day political, cultural and economic interests, rather than a transcendent font of beauty, wisdom and values. Where traditionalists understand Shakespeare as a beautiful remote star, cultural materialists see his plays as trees, growing from the soil of political concerns in the world. They absolutely reject all the 'traditional' claims made for Shakespeare's plays.

Is Shakespeare 'simply the best'?

To begin with, they oppose the 'aesthetic worth' argument and deny that Shakespeare is 'simply the best'. In addition to suggesting that 'the best' in literature is not as straightforward as it seems – Whose best? Who decided? Why? – the cultural materialists have two arguments. First, they describe the development of Shakespeare's reputation, showing that the idea of Shakespeare as the 'best' is not the result of the quality 'shining through' but instead the result of historical events. Second, they compare Shakespeare's reputation with the reputation of other writers to highlight the elements of historical chance.

The story of how Shakespeare the Playwright became Shakespeare the Institution is a long one, and there are a number of easily available sources that cover it in detail (see 'further reading'). Roughly, it suggests that, although Shakespeare was successful during his career as a dramatist, he was not seen as outstanding. For example, Shakespeare was buried quietly in 1616: in contrast, when his friend and rival Ben Jonson died in 1637, a crowd followed the coffin to St Paul's Cathedral. Historians of Shakespeare's reputation argue that its first boost came in 1660. From 1642 to 1660, during the Civil War and Commonwealth, theatres first in London, then throughout England, were closed as the country's rulers – Oliver Cromwell (1599–1658) and Parliament – considered plays immoral. In 1660, the theatres were reopened. Lacking any recent material, theatre owners and managers were forced back to plays from the past, including Shakespeare. A handful of editions of Shakespeare's plays were brought out by theatre managers for use in the theatre. However, as Gary Taylor points out in *Reinventing Shakespeare*, a very readable study of Shakespeare's changing reputation, between 1660 and 1700 as many as thirty editions of plays by Shakespeare's near-contemporaries Beaumont and Fletcher were published. This shows that Shakespeare was not seen as the most important playwright. Nevertheless, towards the end of the sixteenth century and beginning of the seventeenth, Shakespeare's reputation began to grow. As the market for books grew, editions of Shakespeare grew: there were editions in 1709, 1725, 1733, 1747, 1765 and 1768. In fact, it became quite the thing for somebody with literary ambitions to edit Shakespeare as a marker of their own importance and seriousness.

By the beginning of the nineteenth century, the growth of the Romantic movement in the arts helped to foster Shakespeare's reputation.

Romantics considered the 'creative force' to be vitally important, and they saw Shakespeare as a leading example of creativity. His work was read more widely and the characters of his plays began to take on their own life. As Henry Crawford, a character in Jane Austen's (1775–1817) *Mansfield Park* (1814), says: 'Shakespeare one gets acquainted with without knowing how. It is part of an Englishman's constitution. His thoughts and beauties are so spread abroad that one touches them everywhere, one is intimate with him by instinct.' Echoing T. S. Eliot (see Chapter 5), it seems that for Crawford, Shakespeare is in an Englishman's bones. The idea that Shakespeare was the central figure of literature, especially English literature, began to grow. The expansion and consolidation of the British empire took Shakespeare's reputation with it and, as Chapter 1 outlined, used Shakespeare to its own ends; his texts became the touchstones of 'Englishness' to which the empire referred. By the beginning of the twentieth century, Shakespeare had become an icon. In 1910, the British poet Swinburne (1837–1909) wrote that the

> word Shakespeare connotes more than any other man's name that ever was written or spoken on the earth . . . It is not only the crowning glory of England, it is the crowning glory of mankind, that such a man should ever have been born as William Shakespeare.

The use of Shakespeare for patriotic propaganda during both world wars set the final seal on his reputation as the greatest English writer.

Since then, Shakespeare's reputation has been caught up in a snowball effect. As 'everyone' seems to agree that Shakespeare has the highest prestige, people try to associate themselves with 'the Institution' of Shakespeare as a sign of their own value. For example, if an aspiring theatre director wants to show that she or he can be considered highly talented, they take on the 'hardest' challenge of the 'greatest' plays: Shakespeare. Actors often say they knew they had 'made it' when they played their first Shakespeare role. TV series like *Star Trek* use Shakespeare to sound serious or, like *The Wire* are compared to Shakespeare's work. Film studios make 'Shakespeare' films to prove their artistic credentials, or adapt them to show their relevance. And if such people keep demonstrating that they see Shakespeare as the 'best', others will keep believing it.

However, looking more closely at this history of Shakespeare's reputation, the cultural materialists argue that the assumption that Shakespeare is the best relies not simply on the quality of his work but on historical chance. This is highlighted by comparing his work to that of other writers. There are a number of authors who could be considered just as 'great' as Shakespeare but, lacking the support of an empire and all the cultural power of 'England' and 'the English' over four hundred years, they simply don't have the same reputation. The Athenian playwright Sophocles (c. 496-c. 406 BC) had a major influence on the genre of tragedy, but only 7 of 120 or so of his plays survive. The prolific Spanish writer Lope de Vega (1562–1635) was a contemporary of Shakespeare. He wrote many more plays than Shakespeare did, for a similar audience, and they were very popular. Jonathan Bate takes up this case in *The Genius of Shakespeare*, pointing out that 'Spain went into decline and Lope was not translated. The whole of Shakespeare has been translated into a score of languages; less than ten per cent of Lope de Vega's surviving plays has ever been translated into English.' According to Bate, the decline of Spain as a political power led to the failure of Lope de Vega to survive as a 'great world writer'. While the English empire expanded, and took Shakespeare to its colonies, Lope de Vega became less and less well known.

Does Shakespeare teach values?

The second traditionalist claim I discussed was that texts transmit universal values applicable to all people at all times ('not for an age, but for all time'). The cultural materialists oppose this, saying that the time and place in which works were written and are being read are vitally important. A great work isn't 'neutrally' great, but has been acclaimed as great for certain reasons. A cultural materialist might ask, suspiciously, why any particular judgement was made at any particular time, or why that play was popular at that historical moment. One example of this is the popularity of *Henry V*. Interpreted as a patriotic play celebrating British victories abroad in adversity, it was (unsurprisingly) very popular during World War II. Where a traditionalist might argue that Shakespeare speaks to everyone, a cultural materialist argues that class, ethnicity, gender, age, education and so on make a great deal of difference. No text can speak in the same way to everybody: some people might even say the text doesn't speak to them at all.

For a cultural materialist, it is no surprise that both people on the Right and the Left can find their values reflected in Shakespeare. They argue that there is no one 'right' meaning in Shakespeare: we each read into the plays what we will, depending on our world-views. What is interesting to the cultural materialists, if there is no essential meaning or universal value to be sought, is the way in which Shakespeare's plays are *used*: plays can be used to transmit views, as well as reflecting them. In his very accessible and witty books *That Shakespeherian Rag* and *Meaning by Shakespeare*, Terence Hawkes, a leading figure in this movement, argues that there is no 'real' Shakespeare, and his plays are not 'the repository, guarantee and chief distributor next to God of unchanging truths'. 'Shakespeare' is only the name for a cultural tool to convince people of a series of ideas. As an institution, Shakespeare has a great deal of authority – if someone wishes to persuade you of an idea, calling on Shakespeare as evidence seems to give that idea more strength.

Even more interesting is Hawkes' idea that the 'institutionalisation' of Shakespeare makes the plays into ciphers. In *Reinventing Shakespeare*, Gary Taylor compares Shakespeare to a black hole:

> Shakespeare himself no longer transmits visible light: his stellar energies have been trapped within the gravity well of this own reputation. We find in Shakespeare only what we bring to him or what others have left behind; he gives us back our own values.

For Taylor, all the work done on Shakespeare by academics, teachers, critics, students, theatre directors, actors, film-makers and so on has obliterated Shakespeare, and what is left is merely a reflection of their own values. Sometimes it seems that Shakespeare is so much part of our society that we don't even need to read his plays: you can see a film of *Romeo and Juliet* and it will give you an idea of what it's about. You may feel you know the play, but in fact you have seen someone's interpretation of the text, with issues emphasised by the director, because those were important to her or him. If this is the case, you are learning more about the director's values than you are about Shakespeare's play. And if you then read the original text, it may well be harder to interpret it another way, once you have certain ideas – presuppositions – in your mind. There is so much talk about Shakespeare, and so many ideas about the plays crop up in everyday English life, that it is perhaps impossible to think about the text itself rather than what people have said about it.

One important example of this is the way in which Shakespeare – the Institution – is used as a national symbol. Praise has been heaped on Shakespeare for describing the 'English' spirit (paradoxically, this usually occurs at the same time as praising him for being 'universal'). The *Royal* Shakespeare Company is identified with the monarch, the Head of State, and so with the rest of the United Kingdom. A speech from *Richard II* (Act II, scene i), where England is described as

> This royal throne of kings, this sceptred isle
> This earth of majesty, this seat of Mars,
> This other Eden, demi-paradise

is regularly taken completely out of its context and used, with swelling music, in advertisements and in party political broadcasts to help raise a patriotic fervour. Admiring Shakespeare creates a 'we', a sense of shared identity, and to dislike Shakespeare is seen almost as a declaration that you are not 'one of us' and not 'patriotic'. Teaching Shakespeare, the national poet, conveys (somebody's) idea of 'Englishness'. You might also notice that lots of guides to Shakespeare use 'we' throughout – 'through studying Shakespeare we learn', for example, or 'we need look no further'. This seems innocent enough, but any 'we' ('us here') needs a 'they' ('them over there') in order to define itself: Shakespeare is used as a key tool of that definition. It may be wise to wonder about who this 'we' – teachers, students, academics, the government – actually is and what other ideas this 'we' might be passing on to you. This is not to say that the 'we' has always to be elitist. Indeed, in *The Genius of Shakespeare*, Jonathan Bate argues that Shakespeare has been used as a subversive anti-elitist force. As an example, he cites a version of *The Tempest* by the Martinique-born writer Aimé Césaire (b. 1913). In this version, from 1968, the play is retold from the point of view of the slave Caliban. The 'wise old man', Prospero, is seen as a totalitarian slave-owner. Shakespeare here is being used to oppose racism and highlight Europe's slave-owning past.

Another case of Shakespeare reflecting values is the link made between class, education and Shakespeare. For example, a critic called David Hornbrook writes that, for most people, Shakespeare 'is inescapably associated with social snobbery'. Students (especially in school) who enjoy Shakespeare are usually the 'academic' ones, the 'literary A stream'. As this is usually a minority of students, Shakespeare is thus seen as elitist. The central role of Shakespeare in the examination system and its links with success and rewards in education leads to an understanding that Shakespeare divides the good from the bad. Knowing about Shakespeare is a badge of admission into a certain group. It is because the institution of Shakespeare divides as much as it unifies that Fay Weldon's image of Shakespeare as a castle is so apt: a castle means security for those living within, but is imposing and even threatening to those outside. Medieval rulers built castles as a sign of ownership and authority, and aimed to frighten their subjects into submission.

Does Shakespeare have a universal appeal?

Cultural materialists also question the traditionalists' third supposition, that Shakespeare has universal appeal. I have already quoted the journalist James Wood and his belief that it 'is difficult to watch *King Lear* in a theatre and not hear people crying'. In reply, John Yandell writes that the 'reality is, though, that it is very easy to find performances of *Lear* at which no-one cries, at this or any other moment'. Does everybody even understand Shakespeare the first time they read him, let alone have a strong response? There are, as might be expected, formidable resources for helping to teach Shakespeare's plays at college or secondary school, on Access courses and beyond. One example is *Secondary School Shakespeare: Classroom Practice*, edited by Rex Gibson, the director of the effective and useful 'Shakespeare in Schools' project, which aims to bring Shakespeare to life in school. It is full of suggestions and ideas for teaching Shakespeare's plays. Throughout, 'Shakespeare' is invoked: 'Shakespeare isn't neutral'; 'Begin Shakespeare early'; 'How to begin Shakespeare'. Notice how the word 'Shakespeare' is almost a verb and a noun in some of these cases. In the last example, it could mean 'how to begin *to study* Shakespeare and his plays', or 'how to begin *to Shakespeare*'. It ends with an entreaty, 'Trust the students – and trust Shakespeare'. Shakespeare sounds more like 'Disney' or 'Coca-Cola' or 'God' than a 400-year-old playwright. The paradox is, of course, that if Shakespeare did speak to everybody all these efforts to make his work seem accessible and exciting simply wouldn't be necessary. This is not to say that everything you study should come easily, but rather that if it doesn't come easily it may not speak to everyone.

For the cultural materialists, then, it is impossible to get to a 'real' Shakespeare. Moreover, Shakespeare the Institution is never innocent or neutral. More than any other name, more than any other series of literary texts, Shakespeare is *used*. On top of this, he has not even always been considered 'the best' and his plays may only have survived because of historical chance.

The effects of this debate on studying Shakespeare

These academic arguments about Shakespeare's reputation and the way in which the plays are understood have direct effects on the way you 'do' Shakespeare. The United Kingdom National Curriculum takes for granted the 'traditionalist' understanding of Shakespeare. For example, it suggests that students 'should discuss the themes, settings, characters and literary style' of the plays. This is usually translated into studying Shakespeare through plot, character and themes, as any study guide will show. The plot is studied because it is the easiest to understand. The characters are studied because it is assumed that Shakespeare still 'speaks' to us through the characters. And the themes are studied not just because 'doing English' has traditionally concentrated on finding the 'message' in a text, but also because the themes of Shakespeare are 'universal' and so reveal 'universal values'.

However, the cultural-materialist viewpoint brings with it a whole range of fascinating new questions you could use to approach Shakespeare. Some of these questions might focus on how Shakespeare's plays are used – Why do productions of his plays differ? What lies behind the differences in film versions of the plays? Others might explore the cultural power of Shakespeare – Why are quotations from Shakespeare found throughout the British press? Why do so many novels, from all genres, use Shakespearean quotations as titles? Other questions might focus on the editions themselves – Should editors modernise the spelling of the plays or leave it in 'the original'? What is at stake in this choice? Why do teachers tell you to read one edition rather than another?

In relation to the plays themselves, there is an even wider range of questions. In a book for teachers by Susan Leach called *Shakespeare in the Classroom*, the author suggests the following examples:

- Who holds the power in the play?
- What is the economic basis of the play?
- Is the power held/obeyed/challenged/overthrown?

- What is the framework within which the plays operate?
- Is it possible to make easy judgements about the behaviours of any character?
- How does gender work in the play?
- How are women presented?

These questions, which don't take the greatness of Shakespeare or the universal values of his plays for granted, move a long way from the familiar trinity of plot/character/themes.

Another version of this debate appears in a current controversy between two different groups of scholars. On the one had are 'historicists', or 'new historicists', who are keen to put Shakespeare's plays into their historical context, to understand them as works from the past. 'Dramatists are best understood in relation to their time' writes James Shapiro, author of *1599*, a detailed study of one momentous year of Shakespeare's' life. Perhaps the most famous current exponent of this is the critic Stephen Greenblatt, who invented the term 'new historicism'. He not only writes beautifully but consistently places Shakespeare's works into the complexities of his time. For these people, Shakespeare's greatness is interwoven into his context. On the other hand are those who call themselves 'presentists': 'presentism' is used by historians to condemn people of seeing things only from the present perspective, without the correct historical context. In some ways this is a foolish accusation because we can only see things from the past from our current perspective (so all forms of history or context setting are somehow 'presentist'). So in contrast, rather than think of the present as an 'obstacle to be avoided' in our understanding of Shakespeare, 'presentists' think of it as a 'factor actively to be sought out, grasped' and something which we should pay close attention to, as Terry Hawkes writes. This sort of approach not only recognises the artistic power of Shakespeare's plays but also, as Ewan Fernie argues, that the plays require us to be 'responsible', to respond to them. In part, this can mean that, for example, the anti-Semitism of *The Merchant of Venice* is not simply a historical curiosity, but has to be faced; in part it can mean that questions about power and politics posed in *Julius Caesar* still have to be thought through.

This sort of argument, too, exists over the ways in which people think about adaptations of Shakespeare. For some people, the plays exist almost like novels, to be read and cherished; for others, the plays are just that – plays to be performed, acted, changed, as one might change a recipe or improvise a piece of music around a tune. Any performance of Shakespeare is an adaptation of the play text, and some – for example, comic Hollywood films – go much further in improvising than others; indeed, you might ask when a Shakespeare play stops being a Shakespeare play. (Of course, there is no right answer to these questions, but exploring them tells us more about Shakespeare and about ourselves.).

Exploring this debate shows that thinking about what we read, like thinking about how we read, leads to all sorts of questions about how we see the world. Asking 'Why study Shakespeare?' leads directly into questions about the relationship between art and politics, or between literature and history, and is interwoven with important issues like gender, sexuality, class, ethnicity and national identity. Despite being opposed to the traditionalist view, the cultural-materialist approach doesn't necessarily argue that Shakespeare isn't worth studying, or that all artistic values are relative, but it does insist that it's worth questioning assumptions about the poet and the plays. As everybody uses the institution of Shakespeare, from the government to examiners, to the writers of *Star Trek*, it's almost impossible to avoid some contact with it. However, it is vital not just to assume Shakespeare's greatness but also to think about how we construct it. What is at issue is not just the plays but *how we look* at the plays. Meanwhile, the debate goes on – Castle Shakespeare is under constant siege.

Summary

- Shakespeare has become an institution, not only in literature but also in British cultural life. It's almost impossible to avoid the institution of Shakespeare.
- The 'traditionalists' argue that Shakespeare should be studied because of the aesthetic worth of his work, because he communicates values shared by everyone and because he has universal appeal.
- The 'cultural materialists' are more interested in the way the institution of Shakespeare is related to politics and history. They argue that he is considered 'the best' through historical chance, that the values we see in Shakespeare depend upon our own ideas, or those of others who 'use' the institution, and that the plays do not speak to everyone. Cultural materialists argue that Shakespeare is the name for a key cultural tool used to convince people of a series of ideas. Whichever approach you agree with, the debate shows the importance of thinking about how you look at Shakespeare's work.

PART III

READING, WRITING AND MEANING

7

The author is dead?

- Who decides what a text means: the author or the reader?
- What is the traditional view of the author, meaning and the text?
- What are the problems with this view?
- How else can we determine the meaning of the text?
- Why has the author always seemed so important?
- What are the consequences of all of this?

Having looked at how we read and what we read, I'm going to move on to other debates in English that centre on questions of literature, meaning and how we see the world. Chapter 7 is about the relationship between texts and meaning, authors and readers.

How important is the author in deciding what a work of literature means?

At first this might look like a silly question: after all, the writer *wrote* the text and must have meant something by it. However, for literary critics this very question has been the focus of one of the most heated debates of the last sixty years. Roughly, the debate has two sides: those who believe that *authorial intention* – or what the author 'meant' – is central to working out the meaning of a text and those who believe that a text has no fixed meaning and that any understanding depends on the individual *reader's interpretation*. Perhaps the most influential figure on this second side of the debate was the French writer and critic Roland Barthes (1915–1980), who wrote an article called 'The Death of the Author'. While the whole discussion is more formally known as the debate over the 'intentional fallacy' or over 'authorial intention', it is often referred to as the 'author is dead' debate, in an echo of Barthes's title.

For 'authorial intention': the authority of the author

The Examiners are unanimously of the opinion that the proper interpretation of a first person pronoun in a piece of writing is to take that individual to be the writer unless there is internal evidence to the contrary. This is the only logical course to take. Teachers who urge upon their students the term 'persona' or invite them to use 'safe' phrases such as 'the speaker in the poem' cause their hapless candidates enormous trouble.

(Associated Examining Board Report 1995: 27)

For these examiners, and for many people teaching and studying literature, it is 'common sense' that when a poem is written in the first person, 'I', then that 'I' is the author. They are claiming that any other approach is illogical, and causes confusion. It is even more 'common sense' that what the text means is what its author intended it to mean. However, 'common sense' is often the pretext for taking an idea for granted. If the aim of studying literature is to think about *how* we read, then it is exactly these sort of presuppositions that need to be examined. What, then, are the ideas wrapped up in this 'common-sense' attitude?

Those who share this attitude believe that the text means what the author intended it to mean, and nothing else. The text itself, they imply, is like a code, in which the author has encrypted her or his meaning. In reading, the reader decodes the language of the text to find the ideas the writer has hidden within. A diagram to express this might look like Figure 7.1.

This seemingly simple idea – that reading a poem or a novel, seeing a play, is just decoding what the author intended – makes at least four presuppositions that have profound consequences for the study of English.

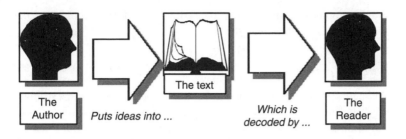

Figure 7.1 **The 'traditional' approach**

(i) Meaning

If a text is understood as the encoding of the author's intention, it leads to the assumption that the text has one definite meaning, just as a code has a definite meaning. Once the reader has cracked the code, they have explained the text and have solved the riddle: they can give a final and accurate account of meaning and there is nothing more to say. However, works of literature often have ambiguous phrasing and seem to offer two or more meanings. Then people who argue this point of view suggest that the author intended to be ambiguous, and meant both things at once (with the implication that she or he was very clever to be able to do that). In general, this assumption leads to essay and exam questions like: 'How does Shakespeare convey the strengths and weaknesses of Othello's character?' If the reader sees Othello as both strong and weak, it is because Shakespeare intended it to be so. The assumption also leads to some interpretations of texts being described as wrong because they are not considered to be what the author intended.

(ii) Biographical evidence

If you accept that what the author intended is what the text means, it seems possible that you could understand a text without even reading it. Imagine finding some evidence – a letter from the author to a friend, for example – that says, 'I mean my novel to be about the conflict between good and evil.' Then you could say: 'This novel is about good and evil. I know this because the author said so!' It would be like seeing the original message before it was put into code. This sort of interpretation, autobiographical criticism, uses the writer's life story, through letters, diaries and so on, to explain the text.

(iii) Authorial presence

All these assumptions rely on the idea that the author is, in some strange way, present in the text, actually there. Through reading the text, you are in direct communication with the author. This assumption leads to questions like: 'In *Paradise Lost* Book 1, does Milton convince you that Satan is both attractive and corrupt?' This ghostly presence of the author is the final 'authority' that can decide what the text means.

(iv) Simple evaluation

Once it is known what the author intended and so what the text means, it is possible to judge the text by how well the author achieved what she or he set out to do. This assumes that judging a work of literature is like judging someone in a race. If you know the sprinter intends to run 100 metres in 10 seconds, you can judge whether she or he fails to live up to her or his intention. If you know what an author intended to do, you can ask questions like: 'How successfully does Jane Austen show the growth of her female characters?'

While many forms of interpretation rely upon this idea of authorial intention, and it might appear to be 'common sense', it has been criticised for a range of reasons. These criticisms are outlined below.

Against 'authorial intention': the death of the author

Throughout this book I have argued that texts are always *interpreted* and open to different interpretations, stemming from readers' different world-views. The idea that by uncovering the authorial intention it is possible to find out the 'true meaning' or the 'right answer' runs directly against this and underlies all the major objections to authorial intention.

(i) Meaning: is literature a code?

Is literature simply a code? Certainly, this is the impression given to many students of 'traditional' English courses, such as the 'old' A-level. It is taken for granted that literature is about something – the 'theme' – and that the job of the student is to discover what this theme might be. So is this really the case?

I would argue absolutely not, for (at least) two reasons. First, the idea is self-contradictory. If literary texts were simply codes, then, paradoxically, literature wouldn't need to exist. Wouldn't it be much simpler to convey a message in a straightforward way, rather than turn it into a work of fiction? Why write a novel to say 'war is evil' when you could just say it, or go on a demonstration, or form a political party, or lobby (or even become) your own representative in government? Of course, there are texts with polemical messages, but when you respond to the message – for example, 'imperialism is wrong' – it's the message or the argument you are responding to, not the work of literature itself.

But there is a more important reason why literature is not simply a code to be worked out. A code works like this: two (or more) people share a cipher where, for example, the letter 'A' is represented by the number '1' and so on. One encodes, using the cipher, and the other decodes, using the same cipher. Thinking back to Figure 2.3 (see p. 24), this cipher represents the 'same way of looking' at a text, so both parties are agreed that 14, 5, 13, 15, 14, 9, 5 is a name in code and not just collections of numbers. But, as I have argued, part of the point of literature is that it encourages different ways of looking at texts, creating different results. So, in fact, reading cannot mean *decoding* the secret message, because there is no shared cipher, no one set of presuppositions we all share. Could you really see a text in the same way as a nineteenth-century author? Or even how your classmates view it? In having 'many ways of looking' we have many different ciphers which lead to many different 'meanings'.

(ii) Biographical evidence

This is also very much open to question. First, reading a letter or diary is not the same thing as interpreting a poem or novel. It would be interesting to find out what a text meant to its author, but that is not the same thing as thinking about what it means to you. Two critics, W. K. Wimsatt and Monroe Beardsley, in a very famous article called 'The Intentional Fallacy' (1946) put it like this:

> In the spirit of a man who would settle a bet, the critic writes to [the poet] Eliot and asks what he meant [in his poem 'Prufrock']

... our point is that such an answer to such an inquiry would have nothing to do with the poem 'Prufrock'; it would not be a critical inquiry. Critical inquiries, unlike bets, are not settled in this way. Critical inquiries are not settled by consulting the Oracle.

Reading a text, interpreting a text, is not an activity that has a right or wrong answer. It is not like making a bet.

Second, whatever the 'oracle' author said is itself another text open to interpretation. A letter saying, 'I intended such and such' is not firm evidence. Not only could it be a lie, plain and simple, but it is also open to interpretation because it is written within a certain historical period, where certain ideas were dominant, and because we, perhaps centuries later, may know things that the author didn't (and, clearly, *vice versa*). Authors might have very astute things to say about their own work, but what they say is only as valid as what a reader might say in determining the meaning of a text. Interpreting their work, an author is doing the same job as anybody else looking at a text. Another way of thinking about this is to ask, 'Who owns words?' Wimsatt and Beardsley, discussing poetry, say that a text 'is detached from the author at birth and goes about the world beyond his power to intend about it or control it'. They argue that authors might shape language, but that ultimately it is public property and readers may make of it what they will. This is not a modern idea: at the end of his long poem, *Troilus and Cressidye*, Geoffrey Chaucer (c. 1343/4–1400) wrote 'go little book, go'. He knew that, once created, the poem was out of his hands, and people were free to interpret it in any way they wished.

If an author's comments about intention are not authoritative, biographies are even less useful, being, after all, only an interpretation of somebody's life. It will certainly inform the reader about the author and her or his period, but will not provide a 'correct interpretation' for a literary text.

(iii) Authorial presence

Authorial presence is perhaps the most difficult assumption to understand. The question 'In *Paradise Lost* Book 1, does Milton convince you that Satan is both attractive and corrupt?' and others like it are, in a way, very confused. For they conjure up the rather worrying image of Milton appearing to you and arguing passionately that *Paradise Lost* Book 1 shows Satan as both attractive and corrupt. Surely, it is the *text* of *Paradise Lost* Book 1 and how you read it that would convince you (or not), rather than Milton himself. A text does not magically bring the author into the room with you – writing is just marks on paper. More than that, the very presence of the writing shows up the *absence* of the author. If the author was actually there, she or he could simply talk to you: the written text itself implies their absence, like an empty chair at a celebratory meal. (Look in this book, and others, at all the moments where the text says 'As I have discussed . . . ' or 'We said earlier . . . '. In fact, none of these things are actually 'discussed' or 'said' at all; they are *written down*. Using the sorts of words that imply real speech is a way of suggesting that the author is actually there, present and talking to you. But this is metaphorical, not real. While you read this, I'm off somewhere else!)

Some critics argue that the author speaks *through* the text, but how could you tell when this was happening? In many novels or plays, several points of view are presented, for example through different characters. Which point of view is the author's? And even if there are passages written in the first person 'I', how do we know if this is the author? It is with such questions that Barthes's essay on the 'Death of the Author' begins. He finds part of a novel where it just isn't clear who is speaking. Is it the author's voice? The voice of a role the author is playing (as the narrator, or as 'the spirit of the age')? Is it always clear who, or what, is speaking? Is the author wearing a mask? Or, suddenly, does the 'real' author appear? His point is that if you are looking for the 'authentic' authorial meaning through a moment where the author 'speaks', it is, in fact, very hard indeed to pin down for certain *where* on the page that moment is.

If writers are absent, how could we ever get to grips with the 'authorial intention'? We can't ask them and we can't even find out if there is a part of the text which was written to tell us 'what they really meant'. With the person irrecoverable, it seems foolish to try to work out his or her intention. Instead, perhaps, we should make what we can of the text.

(iv) Simple evaluation

Apart from the question of what you are to evaluate, if you cannot trace authorial intention, *how* should you evaluate? Who sets the standards? Does the question 'How successfully does Jane Austen show the growth of her female characters?' mean there is some fixed model of how successfully the growth of female characters *should* be shown? Or could you compare Jane Austen to another novelist of the period, Frances Burney (1752–1840), and judge who was better? The idea of judgement implies an objective neutrality that nobody could have and demands that everybody thinks in the same way. While it used to be thought that the job of the critic was to judge what 'great works' were and who the 'great writers' were, it is clear that judging a writer's 'success' is more a result of the way the discipline has developed than a useful task in itself.

With these new ideas in mind, we could redraw the 'traditional' diagram of the relationship between text and meaning as follows (see Figure 7.2).

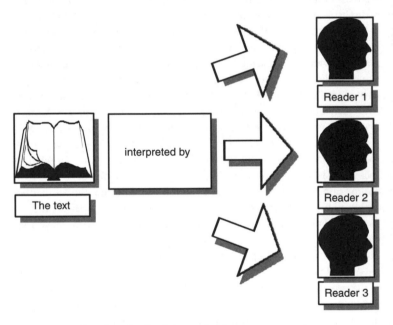

Figure 7.2 **After the 'death of the author' texts are open to interpretations**

The author, in saying what she or he meant by her or his work, can be seen as another reader, with an interpretation only as valid as that of any other person looking at the text. The author is no longer the all-important figure: The Author, as the saying goes, is Dead.

So why has the author always seemed so important?

Those who claim that the author is 'dead' also look at how the figure of the author was 'born', claiming this as another argument against authorial intention. The 'author' and the importance that the role has had in Western European culture was, like all ideas, invented. Of course, with broad concepts and categories of this sort it is impossible to say exactly when it was invented, but it has been argued very convincingly that this idea of the author came into being in or around the eighteenth century. This is obviously not to say that people didn't write before this time, but that their sense of identity as an author and their relation to their texts were different. Mass printing in England began after William Caxton (c. 1415/24–c. 1491/2) introduced the first printing press in 1466 or 1467. Before this, who the author was simply wasn't important for thinking about what things meant. Medieval stories and romances were almost always without named authors (Chaucer is an exception). *Gawain and the Green Knight* is anonymous, but people read it without knowing or caring who the author was. (In contrast, if present-day writers stay anonymous it is precisely because it *does* matter who they are: they might want to escape persecution, or paying taxes, or scandal, for example.)

The concept of the author as the 'true source' of meaning perhaps developed most fully during the eighteenth century: the period of the Industrial Revolution. During this time of massive change, writing became *property*, something that could be sold. It was possible to have a career as an author without a patron, living by selling what one wrote. Since 'ownership' of the words was important to generate income, the importance of attribution grew. Another major influence that fostered the idea of the author was the Romantic movement – a loose collection of poets, thinkers, philosophers and writers in Europe in the late eighteenth and early nineteenth centuries. They focused on the created idea of the writer as *genius*, which didn't just mean 'very intelligent' as it does today. A 'genius' was a person whose immense creative and artistic power was a conduit between unseen powers (of Nature, for example, or the Imagination) and the world of human beings. Not only did this focus attention on the 'author', the genius, but it became important to know who had this special ability and who didn't.

The Romantic concept of the author also stressed that an author must be original. However, some people have cast doubt on the very possibility of originality. Whatever original idea an author might be trying to convey, she or he only has a limited number of pre-existing counters – words – to use to do this, just as an artist has only a certain range of colours to paint with. Even new colours are only mixtures of old ones and although the range of colours is wide – the visible spectrum – it is also limited (try imaging a totally different colour that *no one has ever seen before*). Like colours, none of the words the author might choose are new: words are the only system of meaning that the author can use. If authors want to explain what original idea they 'mean', they can only use words that have pre-existing meanings, so the words will already have *shaped* what the author can say. (This view reverses the normal assumption that an author shapes language: it suggests that, in fact, language shapes authors.) On top of this, much literature is bound by generic conventions, so any work has, to some extent, to fit an already established pattern. In a thriller, for example, the murderer can either be captured or escape. In a way, this doesn't leave much room for originality. These rules can be challenged and changed, of course, but this too relies on the rules, since rebellion has to rebel *against* something. These conventions are not part of the original intention of the author: the 'original' ideas are reshaped by traditions of writing.

So the 'author' is yet another invented category, and even the way this category is defined, as a 'person who communicates original ideas', is open to question. But what are the effects of this?

Consequences of the death of the author

If the author is dead and reading to discover her or his secret hidden intention is no longer the only logical course to take, there are new questions to ask. Perhaps one of the most important would be to ask how one might understand the idea of 'author' now. The 'author' might no longer be the source of meaning in a text, but it doesn't mean that the term has become irrelevant. Knowing about an author does still tell us some things about a text: the French philosopher and historian Michel Foucault (1926–1984) coined the term 'author-function' to describe the way the idea of the author is used. For example, an author's name serves as a classification, as you can be fairly sure what sort of text, broadly understood in terms of style and period, you will find under the name 'Emily Brontë' or 'Stephen King'. This is not to pre-empt the idea of meaning but to suggest that the name is used to group certain texts together. The author-function is also used, correctly or incorrectly, to ascribe value to texts. When, every now and again, somebody claims to have discovered a new Shakespeare poem, there is more fuss than when a new poem by a less famous poet is discovered. Again, if you like the work of a certain novelist, you might buy another novel by the same writer. The author's name also becomes a 'reference tag' for other, often quite vague things like style or themes: critics discuss 'Aphra Behn's style' (1640–1689; British playwright, novelist and translator) or 'Samuel Beckett's philosophy' (1906–1989; Irish writer). Sometimes the names of authors are used as the tags for a whole series of 'big ideas' – 'Darwinism' or 'Marxism', for example. These ideas may have little (or even nothing) to do with those individuals in history, but the ideas still come under the classification of their name, so powerful is the author-function. In none of these cases is the author necessarily a source of authority on the meaning of the text.

The growth of creative writing, as a discipline itself or as part of an AS/A2 curriculum, might also seem to bring back the author, and in some sense it does, as authors can be asked to explore their own work and explain their choices. However, as people work through the intricacies of writing, making choices about words or forms (a sonnet or a free verse poem? A novel or a short story?) or points of view (an all-knowing narrator? Or a first person narrator who is part of the story?), the idea that a single author controls the text that she or he writes seems more complicated as the language and genre itself starts to shape the writing. The choices made in the writing, choices about the form of the text, seem to dictate how the writing proceeds and makes the author less and less all powerful. And, of course, authors when faced with their own texts are readers too, making interpretations of the things they have written.

Perhaps most importantly, the 'death of the author' – or at least of their authority – leads to what Roland Barthes called 'the birth of the reader'. I understand this to mean that a literary work does have a meaning, but it isn't a puzzle or a secret to be found out, placed there in code by a genius author. Instead, it's something that grows as an interaction between the readers and the text itself. Each reader is able – or should be able – to interpret and to produce an array of different and stimulating meanings. You shouldn't be restricted by wondering what the author really meant. The meaning of a text lies not in its origin, but in its destination: in you, the readers. Understanding a text isn't a matter of 'divining the secret' but of actively creating a meaning.

Nevertheless, the author's intention is still endlessly referred to, sometimes to discount perfectly convincing and interesting readings of texts. It seems that many people want to find an authority to explain the text and provide the final answer. It is this wish for a final meaning that links the word 'author' with the word 'authority'. This desire is particularly heightened in reading literature precisely because, I would argue, literature stimulates an unlimited proliferation of meanings. This idea, taken seriously, can seem quite threatening. If thinking about literature makes us think about the world, and there are no right answers about literature, are there any firm answers anywhere?

Summary

- It is often assumed that the author determines the meaning of a text. However, the reader also has a role to play.
- The conventional way of understanding a text as 'what the author intended' makes a number of questionable assumptions about meaning, biographical certainty, authorial presence and evaluation.
- These ideas are open to question: we all read differently, and even authors can only offer an interpretation of their own texts. There is no one fixed meaning to be found or judged.
- The idea of the author is an invention, developed in the eighteenth century.
- The term 'author' does still function as an indication of style, genre or, perhaps wrongly, of quality. However, the meaning in the text relies more on your interaction with it than on the writer's intention.

8

Metaphors and figures of speech

- What is a 'figure of speech'?
- What are metaphors and how do they work?
- How do they affect us?

When you study a literary text, you often concentrate on the way it uses language and 'figures of speech'. It is sometimes assumed that these figures of speech, and metaphors particularly, are just ornaments, there to decorate the texts and somehow show an author's skill. But they are much more important than this: they convey meanings at all sorts of levels, from the most mundane to the very deepest views we hold about ourselves and the world. Doing English involves not just appreciating figures of speech as ornaments, but looking at and questioning their significance.

Figures of speech everywhere

As a rule of thumb, a figure of speech is the use of words or a phrase in a way that isn't strictly true; the words have been 'turned away' from their literal sense and don't mean what a dictionary might say they mean. The technical term for figurative uses of language clearly reflects this: figures of speech of all kinds are called *tropes*, a term originating from the ancient Greek word *tropos*, meaning 'turn, direction, course or way'. There are lots of tropes/figures of speech, and the subject that used to be called rhetoric studied and named all the different sorts. Figures of speech are not restricted to written texts: people use them all the time in everyday conversation. To show how widespread they are, here are seven everyday examples.

When you say something like 'there were millions of people in the room', you are engaging in what is technically called *hyperbole*: an exaggerated statement which everybody knows is exaggerated. If you say 'the book is really good' but mean you thought it was rubbish, you are using *irony*, expressing your meaning by saying the opposite of what you actually mean (of course, people can misunderstand your irony). *Synecdoche* and the closely related trope *metonymy* are two of the most commonly used figures of speech. Synecdoche (pronounced 'sin-ek-duh-key') occurs when people use a part of a thing to represent its whole. For example, when a news reporter says, 'The White House has plans for the economy', she or he is summing up the whole system of US government in the one image of the President's house. When a sailor shouts that she or he sees a 'sail', the word 'sail' stands for a whole ship. (Writers' names are one of the most frequent uses of synecdoche, and we hardly notice it. We say 'Shakespeare' but mean 'Shakespeare's works'.) Metonymy occurs when the name of one thing is given to another thing with which it is associated. For example, when 'the pen is mightier than the sword' means that writing – an activity associated with the pen – is more powerful than fighting – an activity associated with the sword. *Animism* occurs when we describe something inanimate as if it had life; for example, 'the angry clouds'. (This is also known as the 'pathetic fallacy', in the old sense of 'pathetic', which means roughly what we intend by 'sympathetic' – sharing a feeling.) *Anthropomorphism* is rather like animism, but it names the trope that treats non-human things and animals as if they were human. The statement 'my computer hates me' uses anthropomorphism (if we assume that only humans can hate). The British writer George Orwell's (1903–1950) famous satirical novel *Animal Farm* (1945) is anthropomorphic, as are Bugs Bunny cartoons – Bugs (b. 1940) behaves as if he were a person. *Prosopopeia* literally means 'giving a face to' and it refers to personifying things that properly are abstract. If you imagine 'death' as a figure in black with a scythe, or 'war' as a warrior, or describe 'justice' as a blindfolded woman, then you are engaging in prosopopoeia. Because we use them all so often, you might begin to wonder if any phrases aren't figures of speech!

Metaphors in literature

The most widespread figures of speech, *metaphors* and *similes*, are of particular importance for English. Roughly, a metaphor is being used when we say that something *is* something else ('my love is a burning fire') and a simile occurs when we say something is *like* something else ('my love is like a rose'). But how do these actually work? How do they convey meaning?

Like 'trope', 'metaphor' comes from the ancient Greek. It means 'to transfer', which is roughly what metaphors do. Formally defined as the 'application of name or descriptive term to an object to which it is not literally applicable', metaphors transfer meaning by using a term to describe something else. George Lakoff and Mark Turner discuss this in detail in their book *More than Cool Reason: A Field Guide to Poetic Metaphor* (from which many of the ideas in this chapter come). They argue that metaphors *transfer* meaning from one conceptual structure to another and so 'allow us to understand one domain of experience in terms of another'. For example, the first recorded use of the famous metaphor 'the ship of state' ('the state is a ship') was by the ancient Athenian ruler Pericles (c. 495–429 BC). In it 'the state', from one domain (that of politics), is put together with the 'ship', from another domain (the sea), so meaning is transferred between them. The first time you hear the metaphor you might wonder how the state is a ship and what they could possibly have in common, so you think about your concept of a ship. You might decide that a ship needs, say, careful handling during a storm, just as a state needs to be managed during a crisis. Metaphors make us think. Another classic example is 'Achilles is a lion'. Achilles, the celebrated Greek warrior, is understood to be like a lion: very fierce and brave. Achilles is not actually a lion, but we understand his bravery using terms drawn from the natural world.

Traditionally, a simile is different from a metaphor because, where a metaphor says 'Achilles *is* a lion' a simile adds in 'like' or 'as' – 'Achilles is *like* a lion'. However, if we understand the process of metaphor as the transfer of meaning from one conceptual structure to another, there is actually very little difference between these two: they both work in the same way, and because of this the discussion of metaphor applies equally to similes. You could perhaps say that a simile is simply a weaker form of metaphor. It is less powerful to say something shares qualities with something else, – 'Achilles is *as brave as* a lion' – than to say it *is* something else – 'Achilles is a lion'.

In texts that we call literature, metaphors 'defamiliarise' language. The transfers of meaning they make are surprising or disturbing, so the language with which we are familiar suddenly seems unfamiliar. It's this that makes us wonder what the text might mean. The novel *The Go-Between*, by L. P. Hartley (1895–1972), begins with the metaphor, 'The past is a foreign country: they do things differently there.' This metaphor works by using one conceptual domain, geographical space ('a foreign country') to describe another, time. But what does it actually mean to say 'The past is a foreign country'? That we can't speak the language? That we are lost? That we might not be welcome there? That we don't belong there and are only tourists? Is remembering events in one's life like being a tourist? It is this quality of *defamiliarisation* that makes us think. Sometimes, of course, texts use metaphors that are so overused that they are clichés, which don't make us think at all. When we read that 'My love is like a red red rose', we hardly notice it is metaphorical (it is technically a simile) because, since the Scottish poet Robert Burns (1759–1796) used it, it has been used countless times. Roses have become a widely accepted metaphor for love, in literary texts and beyond. When Pericles first compared the state to a ship, his audience burst into spontaneous applause, but today the metaphor goes more or less unnoticed.

Metaphors in everyday speech

The examples so far have been broadly literary, but, as the 'rose for love' metaphor suggests, we use metaphors all the time in our everyday speech. When we say that the 'computers are down' we don't mean that they are literally down, but that they don't work. Likewise, when the singer James Brown (1933–2006) tells us to 'get down', it doesn't mean that we should lie on the floor, but that we should start to dance. (On the other hand, when he tells us to 'get up' he does mean, more literally, that we should get up and dance.) Laid-back people are not always reclining, and, even in the 1960s, cool people were not actually cold. In movies, gangsters 'snuff out' people (you snuff out a candle, so the image is taken from a conceptual domain of lights and lighting) or 'take them out' (leaving life is like leaving a building, or being 'taken out' of an equation). Even when we say that something important is 'central' we are using metaphorical language, transferring meaning from a description of physical location ('central') to describe something's importance. In contrast to the defamiliarisation that literary metaphors give us, these sorts of metaphors are often described as 'dead metaphors'. We take their meaning so much for granted that we no longer even notice that they are not literally true.

Basic conceptual metaphors

Both our everyday metaphors and more explicit literary ones share a characteristic. They tend to build into, or rely on, what Lakoff and Turner dub the 'basic conceptual metaphor' – the underlying metaphorical idea that generates a whole range of metaphors. This is best explained through an example, and Lakoff and Turner discuss at length the basic conceptual metaphor that says 'life is a journey'. Many other metaphors, both literary and non-literary, rely on the basic idea that 'life is a journey'. Lakoff and Turner show how 'The Road not Taken', perhaps the most famous poem by the American poet Robert Frost (1874–1963), relies on this metaphor: Frost sees his life as a journey down one of two roads. Many famous works of literature play with the comparison between life and a journey. For example, the great long poem *The Divine Comedy*, by the Italian poet Dante (1265–1321) begins: 'In the middle of life's road/I found myself in a dark wood'. But this basic conceptual metaphor doesn't just work in literary texts. Pop songs use it all the time. Robert Johnson, the great blues guitarist of the 1930s, sang of 'stones in my passway'. In everyday conversation we use the same basic conceptual metaphor all the time: we 'go ahead' with plans; we get 'sidetracked'; we reach 'crossroads' and 'turning points' in our life; we do things in a 'roundabout way'; like travellers, we are 'burdened with things from our past'; there are obstacles 'in our way'; babies 'begin' the journey and the dead 'rest' at the end. This basic conceptual metaphor transfers meaning from one domain, our experience of journeys, to another, our experience of life. And we are so used to this basic conceptual metaphor that we all know what people mean when they say 'I have reached a crossroads' (even when, in fact, they are sitting quite comfortably at home), or 'the path I must take is clear' (when no track is actually in sight).

Lakoff analyses many other basic conceptual metaphors of this sort:

'love is fire', for example, or 'a human life is a year'. (What season are you in? What season is the oldest person you know in?) 'The past is a foreign country' would be an example of the basic conceptual metaphor 'times are places', where different times are associated with different geographical locations. Each of these basic conceptual metaphors works like an engine for producing new metaphors that are generally understood. Interesting poems, novels and plays (and jokes, advertising slogans or, in fact, anything depending on metaphors) use these basic conceptual metaphors in new, defamiliarising ways. They pull new things out of old models and shake up uses of language we take for granted. Perhaps most radically of all, they can, occasionally, create new basic conceptual metaphors. These have the power to change the way we think about the world and it is this that makes figures of speech, and metaphors in particular, so significant.

What metaphors mean and how they shape the world

So far I have suggested that metaphors are traditionally understood as the point where language 'turns' away from its literal meaning. However, Lakoff and Turner's idea of 'basic conceptual metaphors' changes this completely. These, like 'life is a journey', are so deeply ingrained in us that they are 'an integral part of our everyday thought and language'. Moreover, they have a unique, powerful and fundamental role in leading us to 'understand ourselves and our world in ways no other modes of thought can'. If 'life is a journey', then we can locate ourselves at a point on that journey – at the beginning, for example – and see things that happen in our life as things that happen to us on a journey – obstacles, crossroads, burdens and so on. The problem here is that this basic metaphor, which we so often accept without thinking, smuggles in a number of taken-for-granted ideas that, in general, we might disagree with if they were presented in another form. For example, if 'life is a journey', we might ask if everything that stops you getting your own way is an obstacle. When we have a choice on a journey, it is often a choice of left or right, but in life, is it a choice of one of two options? Perhaps most powerfully, 'life is a journey' smuggles in the idea that life must *go* somewhere, must have a final destination. Does it? The metaphor we choose to use to interpret the world in fact *shapes* how we interpret the world. How we look – the basic conceptual metaphor we choose on purpose or just fall into using by chance – shapes the events we are looking at. If you use a different basic conceptual metaphor, the events may look very different.

Another popular example of a basic conceptual metaphor is less personal and more political. Many people in the United Kingdom and the United States, including some politicians and businesspeople, like to invoke the basic metaphor 'the country is a business'. Once we are convinced of this, it allows all sorts of other decisions to be made that build on the same basic conceptual metaphor. If an employee is found to be stealing from a business, she or he is usually sacked. What policies does somebody who believes that 'the country is a business' support when a citizen ('an employee') of Great Britain Ltd is found stealing? If an employee is no longer able to work, they are made redundant. What would USA Inc do for an 'employee' who could no longer work? Again, the question is which basic conceptual metaphor you decide to use. These basic metaphors control our view of the world. Part of 'doing English' involves understanding their power and analysing them when they occur, to find out exactly what they take for granted. We might begin with literary texts, certainly, but this can stimulate you to look for basic conceptual metaphors in the wider world and to think about the ideas they depend upon. This is part of thinking about the context in which texts are written and understood.

But even more than this, part of the point of doing English, and perhaps part of the point of literature, is to offer new metaphors – not just to surprise us by 'defamiliarising' our normal use of language, but to offer whole new ways of conceptualising the world. For example, it is common to think of knowledge as a tree: there is a trunk ('core subjects', perhaps) and each subject is a branch, subdividing into smaller branches and twigs as the subject becomes more specialised and further away from the trunk. But what if a better and more interesting metaphor for knowledge and learning was not 'a tree' but, as the French philosopher Gilles Deleuze (1925–1995) suggests, 'a rhizome' (a plant like grasses, potatoes or bindweed)? These plants have no centre, no core subjects, but move, grow and change independently of a central authority. Each subject, each clump of grass, would be interdependent, not a 'refined speciality' relying on others. There would be no 'core' subjects that everyone had to acknowledge, but an array of different, and equally valid, sorts of knowledges. The point is that basic conceptual metaphors help determine the sort of things we think, and that doing English helps us to explore and to question these metaphors.

The huge question still remains of *why* we think in conceptual metaphors and why figures of speech are not just ornaments. I suggested at the beginning of the chapter that figures of speech were 'when you use language in a way that isn't strictly true'. Once, in a lecture, I asked what the literal meaning of the metaphor 'He's cool' is. Somebody shouted back 'He's hot!', which made everybody laugh, as one metaphor was simply replaced with another. But there was a point here. The idea of 'coolness' can only be understood metaphorically – there is no literal 'truth' behind it, no actuality that could be unambiguously pointed at, no simple truth from which language could 'turn'. The German philosopher Friedrich Nietzsche (1844–1900) went further. For him there was no 'literal truth' at all: truth is made up from metaphors. He wrote:

> What, therefore, is truth? A mobile army of metaphors, metonymies, anthropomorphisms: in short a sum of human relations which become poetically and theoretically intensified, metamorphosed, adorned, and after long usage seem to a notion fixed, canonic and binding; truths are illusions of which one has forgotten that they are illusions; worn-out metaphors which have become powerless to affect the senses.

For Nietzsche, there is no 'literal' truth that language can convey, and all words in language are really just figures of speech. We think in metaphors and they grasp and control our minds. One contemporary philosopher, Jacques Derrida (1931–2004), describes the way metaphors grasp our mind as 'metaferocity'. We are so used to metaphors and what they take for granted, however, that they have become 'dead' metaphors – 'worn out' and 'powerless' – and they seem to be true. If Nietzsche is correct, the usual understanding of tropes is completely incorrect: they are not 'turnings' of language away from truth, nor just ornaments. Quite the opposite – the figures of speech are the fabric from which the truth of the world is made up. So when we look at the metaphors in a poem, we are, at the same time, thinking about how the whole world is understood.

Summary

- Figures of speech (or tropes) occur when language is used in a way that isn't strictly true. We use them all the time. Metaphors and similes are the most common examples.

- Metaphorical language describes one thing as another ('my love is a burning fire'). It works by transferring meaning, allowing us 'to understand one domain of experience in terms of another'. Literary metaphors 'defamiliarise' language, but we also use metaphors in everyday speech, often without noticing. A metaphor we don't notice is a 'dead metaphor'.
- Both literary and everyday metaphors rely on 'basic conceptual metaphors', such as 'life is a journey'. These work like engines for producing other, generally understood metaphors. Some people argue that these basic metaphors are so deeply ingrained in us that they shape how we see the world. The philosopher Nietzsche argued that metaphors are so taken for granted that we simply think of them as 'the truth' and no longer recognise them as metaphors at all.

9

Narrative and closure

- Why are stories important?
- How do we understand narrative and narrators?
- What is closure?

The last chapter looked at some of the ways in which language was important in texts and in understanding the world. But we also use stories to order the world, and, of course, story – or, more technically, narrative – is what literary texts are made of. A lot of 'theories' or newer approaches to literature draw heavily upon questions of language and meaning, as I discussed in the previous chapter. However, there is also a great deal of work done on the way we use narrative to order and give meaning to our world(s). Doing English means engaging with and understanding narrative.

How are narratives made?

Part of the reason many people do English is that they are swept away by stories. They find books 'unputdownable' and read late into the night. This is part of the power of narrative. It isn't just books, of course. Soap operas, plays, films and in fact nearly every sort of text rely on this narrative drive, the desire to find out 'what happens next'. Narrative is everywhere. It isn't only in fiction: it is also central to each of our lives. When we are born (or at least when we can take notice of what's going on!) we find ourselves 'thrown' into the middle of things and other people's lives. In order to make sense of what's going on, we tell ourselves stories. I'm sure that most of us have – when we were younger – done the same thing as the main character in the Irish novelist James Joyce's (1882–1941) book *A Portrait of the Artist as a Young Man*. At school, he wrote down 'his name and where he was: Stephen Dedalus, Class of Elements, Clongowes Wood College, Sallins, County Kildare, Ireland, Europe, The World, The Universe'. This is a sort of story, about identifying who and where he was. And we are told, and tell ourselves stories about, what has happened to us or who we are and who we want to be, whether we write them down in diaries or transform them into poems or fiction or – more often – just think and talk them through. These stories are how we organise and sort out the chaotic world. They are how we give the world meaning. For example, if you are asked to tell someone about yourself – at a job interview, say – you quickly outline the broad story of who you are, where you come from and so on. You probably would not relate some anecdote from your childhood or describe in agonising detail your morning's journey. You present your story of yourself, organising the narrative and selecting what you take to be the most effective and meaningful facts. This 'organising' is a way of *constructing* the story of yourself: an activity that everybody undertakes, consciously or not.

Because narrative is so important and so all-pervasive in our lives and in the texts we read, study, watch and create, critics have been trying to define and understand it for a long time. A Russian theorist, Vladimir Propp (1895–1970) studied folk tales and argued that each of these fairy stories was put together using some or all of thirty-one narrative motifs. In each one, for example, the 'hero would leave home' or the story would end in a wedding or reunion. In a way, this was just an attempt to make more formal what, in the case of fairy stories, is quite obvious: that Prince Charming from 'Snow White' serves the same function, or does the same job, as 'Prince Charming' from 'Cinderella'. His 'character' as such doesn't really matter (as long as he is charming, of course). What matters is his role in the story as the hero, the rescuer of the heroine from the villains, be they the evil witch or the ugly sisters. The villains, too, are only significant because of their function. Propp's ambition, and the aim of those who came after him, was not simply to analyse fairy stories, but to create a 'science' of narrative, or narratology. This would be a way of breaking down all narratives in all forms into their constituent parts. There have been many rigorous attempts to do this.

These attempts have had some useful results. Certainly, this 'scientific' approach to narrative generated some quite precise terms. For example, one term that is quite widely used is 'diegetic': this is a more formal way of specifying the 'world of the story'. For example, the London Borough of Walford exists in the diegetic of the soap *Eastenders* and Springfield exists in the diegetic world of *The Simpsons* but not in the real world. However, this project does seem flawed in a number of ways. In looking for general laws of narrative, narratology passes over the individual nature of specific texts and is interested only in functions. While this is fine for simpler forms of narrative (fairy tales, or rather formulaic fiction, say), it seems to miss out much that is valuable from other forms of text. It is also 'blind' to historical difference: as both Shakespeare and *The Simpsons* rely on narrative, narratology treats these two art forms from different periods, media and genres as if they were the same. Moreover, each attempt to analyse the text has a position with presuppositions: Propp chose to look at 'the actions of characters', while another narratologist, Gérard Genette (b. 1930), chose to look at the ways a novel uses time, exploring how the 'action' jumped backwards and forwards (with 'flash backs' or what he called analepsis and 'flash forwards' or prolepsis). However, these approaches are neither natural nor scientific but arbitrary. One could analyse a novel in terms of *where* the narrative takes place and how the characters move, rather than *when*, for example.

However, this approach did focus interest on some specific issues. Perhaps the most important of these is the question of narration; that is, who is telling the story?

Narrators

While not all stories have narrators, most do, and most literary texts certainly do. Sometimes the narrators are inside the diegetic, that is, inside the world of the story. Often these are 'first-person narratives' in which 'I' tell the events that have happened to me, or 'voice overs' in a film. *Heart of Darkness* by Joseph Conrad (1857–1924) is a 'first-person narrative' as is the film developed from it, Francis Ford Coppola's *Apocalypse Now!* (1979). But if one person is telling you a story, this immediately raises questions of narrative reliability. How far can you trust the narrator of a 'first-person' story? After all, they don't know what the other characters are thinking or doing, and they are surely telling you what they think is important, and what they think is going on. It is easy to imagine a novel in which what the first person narrator tells us is going on and what is actually happening are different. Indeed, in both *Heart of Darkness* and *Apocalypse Now!* there are 'slips' between the narrator and the story they are telling, leading readers and viewers to suspect that the first person narrator isn't being entirely honest. For example, Marlow, the main narrator in *Heart of Darkness*, describes the vile activities of the Europeans in the Congo and yet seems unwilling to face – clearly – his own complicity with them. (Perhaps it is precisely this struggle between his need to 'confess' and his unwillingness to do so that gives the novel its particular and peculiar form.)

Sometimes, however, the narrator is outside the diegetic, and seems almost to disappear from the story that they are telling. This is 'third-person' narration in which he, she or they – that is the characters – do things that the (nameless) narrator describes. These sort of narrators are often described as 'omniscient', all-knowing, because they do seem to know everything. They can, quite literally, get into the head of the characters and tell you if they are afraid, happy, or if they are hiding something. Traditionally, most novels have this sort of narration: it is the narrator who begins *Pride and Prejudice* by Jane Austen (1775–1817) with 'It is a truth universally acknowledged that a single man in possession of a good fortune, must be in want of a wife' (but is the narrator being *ironic*? Even omniscient narrators are characters).

However, omniscient narrators do not narrate everything. Indeed, part of the power of narrative – 'first-' or 'third-person'- lies in the 'focalisation' of the narrative on or with certain characters. For example, a detective in a murder story may not be the narrator, but the narrative accompanies her or him, rather than, say, one of the bystanders, and only reveals what the detective finds out. The narrative often takes one person's side over another, for example, and who or what the narrator focuses on is very revealing. The story of a murder and its solution told from the point of view of the murderer would certainly be an interesting read, but would it be a detective story? The use of focalisation is very significant, too, in the way it can change what we think about a story. For example, in an adventure story, the narrative focuses on the hero, not on, say, the hapless guard shot dead by the hero in the third chapter. But if the focalisation showed that guard to be a character too, with his own hopes and fears, perhaps the story – and the murderous hero – would look very different. Perhaps the guard works for the villain because he needs the money for an operation for his ill mother, or because he comes from a poverty-stricken part of the world, and the hero simply guns him down. These choices of narrative focalisation shape the meaning of the text. Thinking about focalisation in this way is not 'new' but it does offer new ways to think about texts. For example, although *Heart of Darkness* is set in Africa and is in no small part about the colonial relationship between Africans and Europeans, and even though there are African characters, at no point is the narrative 'focalised' through an African character: the reader is never allowed 'inside their head'. Once this is clear, then other aspects of the novel and its context come more clearly into view.

Closure

However, these ways of analysing and understanding narrative don't seem to explain either its importance or why we find narratives so compelling. This is because they don't deal with the issue of closure. How irritated are you if you miss the end of a TV drama or the last few minutes of a football game or an episode of a soap? How irritated would you be if somebody cut out that last chapter of a book you were reading? Why would you be irritated? Because you wouldn't find out how it ended. This 'wanting to know how things end' is absolutely vital for all stories, from the longest Victorian novels to the shortest cartoons to the most recent Hollywood blockbuster. It is one of the most important things about literature and about life and it is called *closure*.

Here's a test to see how significant closure is: would you read a book or see a film if you knew that the end was missing? Probably not. This shows not only how important closure is but also how the ending of a story is already implicit in its beginning: because even right at the beginning a story has an end, a goal, a conclusion in mind. Stories are *teleological*: they begin with an end in mind. Despite the fact that it is so important, closure – this 'wanting to know how things end', this feeling of teleology – is quite hard to pin down and, like many things in English, it is often just 'taken for granted'. (For example, the basic conceptual metaphor discussed in the last chapter – 'life is a journey' – is a teleological metaphor: by suggesting that a life is a journey it implies that there is a final destination which will provide closure for 'life's story'.) However, although we may not be able to offer a strict definition of our desire for a 'sense of the ending' (as a famous book by the British critic Frank Kermode named it), it is possible to see closure at work. Characters on TV often say that they need closure in their life ('I need closure in my relationship with Ross'). They mean that they need to finish one part of their life, tie up all the loose ends so that they can move on. And in everyday life, there are many events that are 'acts of closure'. Graduation Day at school or university is an event that marks the end, the closure of a part of your life. Funerals don't end the mourning, but they end the immediate period of grief after someone has died. We feel that these acts 'close a chapter'. This is a key idea in understanding closure: we *construct* closure just as we construct narratives of ourselves.

This is why closure is also one of the links between the stories we read or see and our own lives: they both rely on closure to make sense. This is how the American novelist Henry James (1843–1916) put it:

> Really, universally, relations stop nowhere and the exquisite prob-lem of the artist is eternally to draw, by a geometry of his own, the circle in which they shall happily appear to do so . . . He is in the perpetual predicament that the continuity of things is the whole matter for him, of comedy and of tragedy; that this continuity is never broken, and that, to do anything at all, he has at once intensely to consult and intensely to ignore it.

What this means is that things ('relations') keep on going on (your school or college will still be there after you leave) and what artists do is decide how to 'draw' the events, what bits to choose and where to end. In this sense, we are all artists whenever we tell a story. Life goes on, with its continuous events and all stories, fictional or real, are made by decisions about where to end. Do you stop telling the story at the couples' wedding? (a happy ending)? Or at the new husband's fatal car accident (a very sad ending)? Or the widow falling in love again (happy) but being broken hearted when her new love leaves for Africa (sad)? And so it goes on. For Henry James, the artist's choice is where and how to end, how to construct a sense of closure.

Nearly all texts use closure – it's how all stories work after all! Some end with a very satisfying 'tying up of loose ends': the murderer is caught, the wedding happens, or the main character dies. Others are less final and, in recent years, some texts have purposely tried to avoid 'closure' by leaving lots of loose ends, unfinished plots and so on. An example of this is the short novel *The Crying of Lot 49* by the American novelist Thomas Pynchon (b. 1937). This novel in part concerns what might or might not be a massive conspiracy that the central character investigates: but she never actually discovers whether it is a conspiracy or whether she is imagining it all. The point seems to be that not only is closure sometimes a bit hackneyed, but to draw attention precisely to the way in which it is constructed, especially in fiction. But these sorts of novels only work because you expect closure, so they, too, are using closure, but in a different way.

Closure is a key term for studying literature and is vitally important for thinking about how the content, form and structure of a text shape its meaning. Knowing about closure allows you to compare different novels, poems and plays by looking at how they 'achieve closure', which means, really, how their stories work. You might ask yourself how a thriller 'achieves closure' compared with a historical novel, for example, or how conclusive the ending actually is.

The question remains of why our need for closure is so strong. Why do we want to know what happens? There is no, one answer to this, but much of the critical theory you will encounter in higher-level English studies will examine the issue. Frank Kermode suggests that, perhaps, because we know how the story of our own life is going to end – the way all lives end – in death, the endings of the stories we read or tell are like 'little deaths' that will allow us to come to terms with our own, real death. It might also be because closure is a way of constructing and imposing order on a chaotic world, a way of drawing our own circle.

Of course, 'doing English' is not immune to the desire for closure. The desire to come up with the right answer or the final interpretation is in part the desire for 'closure': the end of studying this book or that play. However, if closure is constructed, so are our readings and interpretations that rely on closure. Closure is unavoidable and necessary but, at the same time, has to be seen for what it is: a way of finishing a story or – in the case of doing English – finishing with a story. But literature, although perhaps based on closure, has a habit of not letting itself be 'closed up'. Because there are many different interpretations of texts, we know that a sense of closure, of a final answer, is a construct, and that an interpretation can be opened again, reconstructed or deconstructed by different readers in different contexts. So to think about closure is to think about our own reading and the ways in which we impose our own meaning on texts. When you're doing English, the texts might be literary, but we can also think about the ways in which we impose meaning on the 'texts' of our lives and those of others.

Summary

- Narratives are everywhere and are very powerful. We tell stories in order to make sense of the world and ourselves.
- Some critics have tried to develop a 'science' of narrative, which has helped refine discussions of how stories work.
- There are different sorts of narrators. Some narrators are 'inside' the story while others are 'outside', but both sorts of narration shape the meaning of the text.
- Closure is our 'sense of an ending' and is part of all narrative. Some critics suggest that we seek closure to impose order on our lives, or to come to terms with our own deaths.
- In thinking about closure we can also think about the ways in which we try to impose meaning and 'final interpretations' on texts.

10

Creative writing and critical rewriting

- What is creative writing?
- What is critical rewriting?
- How is creative writing marked?
- How has creative writing changed doing English?

When I was a student, I asked a question about sonnets; the lecturer, poet and academic Grevel Lindop astonished me by saying that the best way to really find out about sonnets was to write one. I think I was astonished both by the audacity (that I might dare to write a sonnet! As if I were an author and not like the literary critic I was being trained to become!), but more by the obvious simple rightness of this suggestion. After all, no one learns to swim on dry land. In English, though all reading is active, creative writing particularly stresses *heuristic* learning: heuristic means learning by doing, finding out, rather than being told or by simply analysing.

What is creative writing?

English is a constantly changing and developing subject, and one of the very biggest changes in recent years, following this sort of idea, has been the explosion in courses offering Creative Writing, either on their own, or (more often) as part of an English degree or AS/A2 qualification. These focus on you as a writer, *doing* writing, as much as on you as a reader.

In a general sense all the texts studied in the discipline of English are 'creative'. But 'creative writing' more specifically names the flourishing of a new development in doing English, where students are able not only to study the work of past and current writers but to produce their own creative work. To be *writers*, that is, not only of interesting essays and analyses of texts, but of their own poems, short stories, novels, plays, journals and other literary forms. But what is creative writing? Can people be taught to be authors? Like most questions in English, answering this involves several other ideas. If creative writing is about enabling students to be authors, this too is to beg a question, one that has attracted a great deal of contentious discussion in creative writing, about what an author is, or does.

Some of the appeal of Creative Writing lies, of course, in the figure of the 'author' (which is one reason why the issues I discussed in Chapter 7, about authorship, authority and intention have been so contentious). There is an attraction in the idea of 'being an author', becoming famous, or, perhaps more interestingly, being able to articulate something important about oneself or the world, to *say something*. But this idea of the author, as a sort of 'inspired genius', absorbed in self-expression, has also been a problem for these courses. As I suggested in Chapter 7, the idea of what the author was has changed over time. To some extent, the idea of an author as an inspired figure, able to express the truth about herself, himself or the world is inherited from the Romantic period at the beginning of the nineteenth century. This idea of the author fits very well with current unquestioned ideas about celebrity, in which it seems that famous writers, actors and musicians and so on are assumed to know not just more about writing, acting and music than non-celebrities (which is reasonable) but also more about world politics, life and everything else. But if one believed completely in this idea of what an author was or is – that he or she was an inspired genius – then, of course, creative writing could not be taught and would not be part of English. It would just 'happen' to you. In fact, of course, all writers have learned to write. Writing is not a natural skill: like learning an instrument, it has to be taught, practised developed and so on.

In response to this, then, a contrasting view of creative writing is that it is a discipline that exists as a 'craft', to teach the student the technical skills of writing. In this context, Steve May, in his book *Doing Creative Writing* answers the question of whether creative writing can be taught very clearly. He begins by saying

> You want to write a story. I don't know what your story is about, what genre you want to write it in, or anything else about it. However, because (I believe) stories share common features, I can be fairly certain that if you ask yourself the following questions about your story, it will help you discover its shape and point:
> 1. Who is it about?
> 2. How do they change over the course of the story?
> 3. What do they want?
> 4. Do they get what they want?
> 5. Who (or what) is trying to stop them?
> 6. What are the key events in the story?
> 7. Which event decides whether the main character gets or doesn't get what they want?
> 8. How does it end?
> 9. Which other characters are absolutely essential to the story?
> 10. Where is the best place to start?

These are technical questions about writing and the decisions writers make. In this view, the author works learning a craft, putting together a story, poem or play, and learning the elements that make them up. While this is empowering, however, it does also imply a vocational sense: that someone doing creative writing will end up a making a living as a writer. However, not all creative writing students will make a living as writers and, of course, many students taking a creative writing module in higher education or at AS/A2 may not want to become writers, so to see these courses as professional training – though again, they are to some extent – is not to see them in their clearest light.

In her book on the subject, Michelene Wandor writes that creative writing is a 'mode of imaginative thought'. Here she echoes the wonderful British novelist Angela Carter (1940–1992) who writes 'Oh, hell. What I really like doing is writing fiction and trying to work things out that way'. For Carter, novels were partly 'thought experiments' which tried to explore imaginatively – but not necessarily answer – certain problems or issues, 'to work things out'. However, all subjects one learns and studies are attempts to explore certain problems: physical geography explores why landscapes are the way they are, for example, and the sciences, at their best, need creative and imaginative responses. What is at issue with creative writing is not just that it is a mode of thought, but *how* it thinks, as it were, what its tool are.

The tools of creative writing as a subject are the literature, criticism and theory that are involved with any literary creative act. (Angela Carter again: 'reading is just as creative an activity as writing and most intellectual development depends on new readings of old texts. I am all for putting new wine in old bottles; especially if the pressure of the new wine makes the old bottles explode'.) Creative writing is another important way of engaging with literature, another of the new ideas that are reshaping English as a subject, stressing the *heuristic*, learning by doing. It brings together you, your ideas, what you have read, different and new thoughts and interpretations with 'hands on' experience of writing in a range of different ways.

One of the forms of creative writing that is perhaps the most widely practised in English courses (and not simply creative writing ones) at secondary and university level is called *critical rewriting*. This technique involves taking an established text and reworking parts of it: for example, a scene from a novel could be rewritten from a different perspective, or in a different context. This is not different, really, from what theatre directors or film and TV adaptors do when they stage a Shakespeare play ('what happens to *Hamlet* if we set it in the 1930s?'; 'what happens to *The Taming of the Shrew*, when, unlike Shakespeare, we use women actors?'). More interestingly, this process of creative rewriting can tell us about the original text, about the new format and about their interaction. For example, the Facebook status update version of *Pride and Prejudice* tells us about the Jane Austen's novel by focusing on the key incidents, on contrasting views and on the events of the narrative. But it also tells us about the 'genre' of Facebook Status Updates: it shows, really clearly, for example, the discipline involved in having to say something funny, clever or moving in only a few words. Most interestingly, both the original novel and the 'Facebook rewriting' – and Facebook and Twitter more generally – share a common feature in their use of irony and humour. If people learn new things by reading texts in different ways, they also learn by writing or by rewriting them in different ways.

Creative writing, then, in some part is one of the new ideas that forms part of doing English today. If some of the ideas described as theory focus a little more on *what* texts mean, creative writing focuses on *how* they mean: though, at some deeper level these two – what something means, how it means – are versions of the same question. In an excellent book about new ways of teaching English and creative writing, Ben Knights and Chris Thurgar-Dawson put it this way:

> Many teachers . . . see a value for writing neither in terms of self-expression nor in terms of the making of future Booker Prize winners, but as an educational process that permits deeper engagement with the already written.

They go on to argue that, while the new ideas in English utterly changed the subject – thus, the need for this book – the way the subject was taught, and what students actually wrote, has not yet been changed. Creative writing and critical rewriting is about changing not only what students think but also what they do: not only to produce essays but also different sorts of heuristic responses to literary texts, ideas and thoughts. In this, the creativity of writing and the creativity of reading are really revealed as the same thing: the best creative writers are also the best creative readers. 'Creative writing' is 'Active reading'. In this way, creative writing and critical rewriting are changing the nuts and bolts of how English is studied and taught.

Nuts and bolts and assessment

Changing the nuts and bolts of English means, among other things, changing how work in English and in creative writing is marked, and one of the questions that has often been asked about creative writing, especially in education, is how it might be assessed.

On the one hand, 'creative writing' is assessed and valued all the time; newspaper or internet reviews judge novels, poems and plays, people who teach courses choose the most interesting books they can, we recommend (or don't) books or TV programmes to our friends. As I suggested in writing about the canon in Chapter 5, you can't escape literary value. On the other hand, it is very hard to imagine giving actual marks to great poets. People involved in creative writing have spent a very long time thrashing out these issues, and the answer again turns on the heuristic and practical. To begin with, much of the work done by students in this area is divided into two: a 'creative' part – the poem, short story, film scene – and a critical or reflective part.

Perhaps ironically, in order to assess the first, 'creative' part, teachers have provided very detailed assessment criteria, focusing on relevant issues to the writing:

- How effectively the piece presented explored the point of view of the main character?
- How clearly has the plot been advanced in this scene?
- Does the choice of rhyme scheme (or lack of rhyme scheme) suit the subject?

In turn the critical and reflective part might be, for example, an essay on the technical features (say, the sort of tropes, following Chapter 8 your creative piece might have used, and why you chose those), or a piece laying out the aims of your creative work and assessing how far you were successful, or an discussion of how you saw your creative piece about growing up in London in the wider context of other novels and stories about childhood.

If the main form of assessment for creative writing has been the creative work together with some reflective work, the main form of teaching creative writing has been the workshop or seminar. The novelist and creative writing teacher Douglas Cowie writes that a

> Creative Writing Workshop is usually run in part or in whole as an opportunity for student writers to submit work-in-progress for consideration by their peers, under the guidance of an experienced writer. A student's work will be read by each member of the group, either during the workshop or beforehand, and the group will then discuss the poem, story, novel extract or play, offering constructive criticism about how the piece does and doesn't achieve its aims, and also offering suggestions for improvement of the piece. There are a number of variations on how creative writing workshop discussions can be run, and in my own teaching I've organized them in different ways depending on (among other things) the experience, size and ability of the particular group. However, the basic foundation of a student's work-in-progress receiving oral and/or written feedback from his or her peer group under the guidance of a more experienced mentor is common to most workshops.

Like much in English, the creative writing workshop is controversial and can, of course, be difficult; some of teaching creative writing is about how these sessions are managed. However, workshops do also reflect an interesting and often forgotten thing about writing itself. While the image of the writer is of a lone person creating by themselves – and there are writers that fit this stereotype – usually writers are involved in communities of different sorts. Novelists and non-fiction writers have friends and competitors (often the same people) to whom they show drafts, as well as editors (*wonderful* editors, as my editor Polly Dodson suggests I add here) and publishers who look at their work and make suggestions. Writers for the stage, TV and film have many collaborators from (one hopes) the informed and sympathetic directors to (one fears) the less scrupulous people for who art is simply another business. Poets read to each other, attend events, festivals, form supportive groups, compose manifestos and make aesthetic friends and enemies to help shape their own writing. The creative writing workshop is a version – perhaps a delimited and controlled version – of these different and jostling communities, so doing creative writing is also about learning how to be in these communities.

Creative English?

To paraphrase Ben Knights and Chris Thurgar-Dawson again, creative writing/critical rewriting should enable you, students doing English, as writers, allowing you to use not only a range of genres but also the fullest range of new ideas about literature and interpretation in as full a way as possible – to say more, perhaps, and understand things that the more traditional forms or writing could not. But these changes have an impact on all the other parts of the subject of English too. Paul Dawson in his book *Creative Writing and the New Humanities* discusses 'Fictocriticism' or 'personal criticism', a sort of criticism that draws more and more on the personal voice and on personal responses to texts. But, at its root, all responses to literature are our own, reflected on, evaluated and changed by all we have learnt and thought. You might not need to invoke a personal voice, or (as the eminent Shakespeare critic Stephen Greenblatt does) tell a story about one's father to be creative in your responses. Another great twentieth century critic, Geoffrey Hartman, argued as long ago as 1980 that 'all criticism entails a rethinking, which is itself creative. . . in every aspect of learning and life'. Because of this, like creative writing, other sorts of ways of responding to texts, other sorts of literary criticism 'may cross the line and become as demanding as literature'; criticism is 'an unpredictable and unstable genre' not limited to a commentary on literary texts. All responses to literature are creative.

Summary

- English is a constantly changing and developing subject; one of the very biggest changes in recent years is the growth of Creative Writing.
- Creative Writing focuses on you as a writer.
- A creative writer is not an 'inspired genius' or simply following a craft, but someone learning about and responding to literature in a different, more heuristic way.
- One form of this is critical rewriting, which involves reworking on already existing text or part of a text.
- Creative writing is often assessed by both a piece of creative work and a piece of reflective work.
- Creative writing stresses the creativity at work in all responses to literary art.

PART IV

ENGLISH STUDIES . . .?

11

English, national identity and cultural heritage

- Why is English involved with 'national identity'?
- Where does your national identity come from?
- How does your national identity affect you?
- What is 'cultural heritage', and what has it got to do with English?
- How are English and national identity changing?

English has been understood by many as the study of the 'national' literature or even of the 'spirit' of Englishness. Less grandly, Brian Cox (a key figure in the development of English as a subject since the 1960s) wrote that 'English is intimately involved with questions about our national identity, indeed with the whole future ethos of British society. The teaching of English . . . affects the individual and social identity of us all.' In 'English', ideas about nation, language and culture meet, mix and become indistinguishable from each other. But how and why is English related to these ideas about national identity? This chapter explores the complicated interaction between English and ideas about how people understand themselves in a wider world of states, countries, ethnicities and peoples.

Where does your national identity come from?

It was once commonly believed that your nationality was in some way part of your body – in your genes, bones or, more romantically, 'in the blood'. But few people now believe this. If it were true, it would be impossible to change nationality, as it is impossible to change the basic codes in your DNA. It would also be impossible for new nations and states to emerge; but, of course, they have done and continue to do so. (People who still claim to believe that 'nationality is in the blood' often do so for very unscrupulous reasons: many of those who were involved in the murderous 'ethnic cleansing' in the Balkans claimed to believe this, stating that, although people had lived in the same place for generations, they were not 'really' from there.) Since nationality is not 'in your blood', it cannot be defined by race or ethnicity, as is sometimes suggested. Indeed, many people now argue that the idea of defining and categorising somebody principally and exclusively by race arose in the eighteenth century. This is not to say that differences between peoples weren't previously noticed, but that these differences weren't seen as summing up all a person was. This idea of 'race' was used to support the growing nation-states and also to 'justify' the unjustifiable evil of slavery. Ethnicity, then, can't be the defining characteristic of a nation. Further, your national identity is not made up simply by passports, rights and citizenship, although these are obviously important.

The book *Imagined Communities* (revised edition 1991) by Benedict Anderson offers a crucial insight into national identity and the idea of a nation. He argues that nations are created, or constructed, *culturally*. They are, in his key phrase, 'imagined communities'. Nations are 'imagined' in two senses. First, they are 'imaginary' communities because, despite any nationalistic rhetoric, they cannot be a real community; simply, they are too big for any one person to know any but the smallest fraction of the total population. Even in a smallish town of 50,000 people, it's hard to imagine one person knowing everybody. In the United Kingdom, with a population of nearly 60 million people, even meeting everybody just once would be impossible. Second, and more important, nations are imagined because they exist *in the imagination*; they are put together with images and ideas. There is no 'real' national identity, no 'essence' to being English or Colombian or Kenyan. Instead, there is a shared stock of images, ideas, stories and traditions, all of which go together to help each of us 'imagine' (and so identify) ourselves as English, Colombian, Kenyan. These shared images, stories and ideas are national culture. The rest of this chapter expands this idea.

Anderson suggests that 'imagined communities' have three characteristics.

1   They are *limited* in size and number. Each nation defines itself through a perception of difference from other nations; the difference between 'us' and 'them'. This means that not even the most power-hungry nation wants to consume all others and be one huge 'mega-nation'. The British Empire never said that New Zealand or India were part of the *nation* of the United Kingdom. They were separate nations, within one empire. Anderson suggests that these borders are not just geographical, but divide nation from nation, 'them' from 'us' in the imagination.

2   Each nation is *sovereign*, claiming to be the institution with final legal authority over its citizens. This is one reason transnational institutions like the United Nations or the European Union are so fraught with controversy.

3   Each nation *imagines* itself to be a *community of people who share something*. An imagined community binds people together in an imagined 'we'. Whether anything is actually shared or not, nations foster the idea that all those who claim to be of that nationality lay claim to something in common. This idea of community implies a deep comradeship, crossing over boundaries of class, race, gender, education, upbringing, religion and so on.

How does your national identity affect you?

The idea of the national 'imagined community' and its characteristics is often taken for granted despite its importance in much of our contemporary life. Your national identity is not just a question of which team you support on big sporting occasions, nor is it simply the symbols on your passport. It also affects how you behave, your expectations, your relations with others and, more importantly perhaps, others' relations with you. It affects what language you speak, how you understand the world and your place in it – it affects the presuppositions you have when you read. Your national identity, in no small way, *makes up who you are*. And because this national identity is 'imagined' it is actually made out of cultural ideas and images. It is usually assumed that your nationality creates your culture, as if the tree of culture grew from the soil of national identity, but, in fact, *it is your culture that creates your nationality*. Culture is a vital component – if not *the* vital component – of national identity.

In his book *Keywords* (1976), the influential critic Raymond Williams (1921–1988) wrote that culture is 'one of the two or three most complicated words in the English language'. The word has at least three different, but interwoven, meanings. The first is personal: to be 'cultured' is to have undergone a process of learning and development (to be, as the founders of English might have phrased it, 'civilised'). The second meaning refers to culture as 'high culture': the great (that is, canonical) works of literature, opera and classical music, for example. The final meaning refers to culture as a word to sum up a much wider array of things: images, objects, pictures, comics, 'pulp' literature, religious ceremonies, pop songs, films, clothes, television, soaps, football team histories, traditions, and everything else that goes to make up the world we experience. This meaning of 'culture' makes up what Homi Bhabha (a leading contemporary thinker on culture and nationality) calls 'the scraps, patches, and rags of daily life', all the made things and invented ideas through which we live and that make up our identity. The culture that creates 'imagined communities' is not only what is called 'high culture' but, perhaps more importantly, is also culture in this wider sense.

This is because national identity is not something that is laid over your personal identity, as if you were a blank canvas with a nationality painted on top. To ask which came first, the personal identity or the national identity, is to ask a chicken-and-egg question. Our sense of national identity plays a central role in constructing us *and* it is something we ourselves construct. Bhabha argues that people are both the *objects* created by national identity and the *subjects* who, in turn, create it. We are objects of it because we are *constructed* by our languages, histories, location and so on – our culture – but we are also subjects because we *act out* national identity in all sorts of ways, usually cultural. We create it as it creates us. So Bhabha argues that national identity is both *pedagogical* (taught to us at home, at school, in the community) and *performative*, performed, acted out and 'done' by us in all sorts of ways. Obvious ways of performing your nationality, or acting out a national culture, might include supporting a national sporting team or being involved in a nationwide event, such as voting in an election, watching a royal wedding or funeral on TV, for example, or celebrating a named national holiday such as Independence Day, Bastille Day, Guy Fawkes night and so on. Smaller ways might include watching a TV serialisation of a 'classic of English literature', or a soap showing the daily lives of 'typical' English people, visiting a 'national landmark', or even handling money, which is stamped all over with national symbols. Even the simple fact that you have to fill in a 'Nationality' box when applying for a driving licence enacts your national identity. All these acts both define you and are examples of you defining yourself. Being taught and studying a subject called not 'literature' but 'English' is a very significant way of defining and being defined by a national identity.

English as cultural heritage

It is at this point that the idea of cultural heritage becomes important. The imagined community keeps what it values from its past: tangible things, like stately homes, museum exhibits, battlefields and so on, as well as intangible things like stories, attitudes, ideas and beliefs. 'Heritage' in this sense is made up of the cultural things that shape the 'we' of the imagined community and, significantly, is a version of how the community wants to see itself. (The question this begs, of course, is who decides what is and isn't 'heritage', and why. For example, why are lots of stately homes from the eighteenth century preserved, but hardly any workers' cottages or district poorhouses?)

There is, of course, a huge array of different ways of presenting cultural heritage. In some countries, the stories of, for example, their nation's founding and their national heroes are central. But what is central to 'English' (the identity and the discipline) is not the material items of cultural heritage, like Jane Austen's house or Queen Victoria's chair, or even things like 'Dickens' London' or 'Shakespeare country'. It is rather the intangible shared stories, attitudes and ideas that 'everyone should know'. It is these that make the subject 'English' so crucial for ideas of national identity. Stories – like Shakespeare's plays, for example, or the novels of Charles Dickens – make up a reservoir of tales, ideas, images and values constructing and strengthening the idea of the English imagined community. You don't even have to have read one of Dickens' novels to be aware what the adjective 'Dickensian' means, or to know that a 'Scrooge' is a miserly person. Again, this takes for granted the idea that works of literature contain values, messages or morals on which 'we' – the imagined community of the English – could all agree. Once 'we' have agreed on those, it would then (in principle) be easy to agree on an array of other, possibly more troublesome and more 'real', issues.

However, as I have argued throughout this book, reading is as much about how we look as it is about what we look at. This 'shared agreement' about 'values, messages or morals' is not one that arises from having novels, plays or TV programmes in common or even from admiring the same monuments. It comes from being taught to *interpret* them in the same way. 'We' are still being taught how an 'English person' looks at things, in a clear echo of the way the teaching of English developed in India to make people more 'English'. This means that it isn't so much a shared knowledge of, for example, Dickens, that is our literary heritage, but rather the way in which we have been taught to *understand and interpret* Dickens. English as a subject teaches you a way to look at things. In the way it makes you produce essays, projects and ideas, it teaches (and, through assessment and exams, enforces) a way of making you act out this 'English' method of looking. English as a subject is a form of cultural heritage, aiming to help create a 'we' by making us read and interpret in the same way. Because the subject is compulsory at school and is also highly regarded, it is a particularly strong way to bind people together.

This is one of the reasons people find the idea of 'theory' quite threatening to culture and national identity. If theory is, as I have argued, a range of different ways of looking at things, it means that the 'English' way of interpreting literature is no longer unique. 'Theory' is seen as a threat not just because it offers new interpretations of texts, but because it offers new ways of looking. New ways of interpreting don't construct the same 'we' as before; in fact, they both teach and produce new forms of national identity.

Theory and multicultural heritages

Despite the power of the 'we', there is *not really any one single culture* that everyone inhabits. A single national identity is always the *result* of a binding-together and the 'we' of a national culture is built up by the interaction of lots of different cultures. With very rare exceptions (communities isolated by historical accident or through their own choices, for example) this has always been the case. However, importantly, the modern world is characterised by even more interaction between cultures than ever before – some people describe this as part of the process of 'globalisation'. We now inhabit a *hybrid* society where different cultural traditions, ideas and assumptions try to rub along together. They might all share a nation, but people brought up in different places, either within or outside the national boundaries, people brought up in different classes or in different ethnicities or with different religions or expectations, have, to a greater or lesser degree, different cultures. Although this is sometimes seen negatively as the cause of friction, 'multicultural' mixing can also be a fantastic benefit. Salman Rushdie (b. 1947) is a novelist whose work explores this mixing of an array of cultures (his 1981 novel *Midnight's Children*, about Indian Independence, was judged to be the best Booker prize winner in the first forty years of the competition). He wrote that his work

> celebrates hybridity, impurity, intermingling, the transformations that come of new and unexpected combinations of human beings, cultures, ideas, politics, movies, songs . . . Mélange, hotchpotch, a bit of this and a bit of that is *how newness enters the world.*

It is worth remembering that, at the beginning of the twenty-first century, the favourite place to eat out in the UK is the local 'Indian' restaurant, which offers versions of Indian dishes modified (or *hybridised*) for the British market, and the UK's favourite music derives from a mixture of American, African, European and, more recently, Asian models. Rather than insisting on a single imaginary 'national culture', it is more accurate to discuss the mixing of an array of cultures in an ongoing conversation of national cultures. And, if different cultures are mixing and conversing more and more, most importantly, this means that different ways of understanding and thinking about texts must also emerge and mix.

Even though there isn't, and perhaps never has been, a single national cultural heritage, this has never stopped attempts to create such a core for an 'English' imagined community. Traditionally the subject 'English' has been one tool to make everybody from an array of cultures interpret, and therefore see things, in the same way (a way that many have identified with the white male straight English middle class). The term 'heritage' is often used disparagingly, summoning up images of crinoline skirts, obedient servants and steam trains – a 'golden England'. English as a subject, so long as it maintains its attempt to reduce different perspectives, risks becoming a 'heritage' subject, as dated as the telegraph and the corset.

Yet now perhaps this idea that everyone should share a single monolithic heritage has started to adapt and change; slowly, sometimes painfully, sometimes with great joy, we are developing a multicultural heritage, or multicultures. And this in turn changes how we imagine our national identities and thus how we teach and perform them. Our sense of 'we' is changing. The study of literature and language could be an opportunity to understand and to encourage an even more open multicultural society. Things in the subject certainly have begun to move this way. The curriculum we study and teach now includes books by writers like Maya Angelou (b. 1928), Alice Walker (b. 1944), Anita Desai (b. 1937) and Chinua Achebe (b. 1930); writers from outside the conventional canon, and outside 'England', who have broadened horizons slightly. A number of widely studied contemporary writers, like Zadie Smith (b. 1975), Michael Ondaatje (b. 1943), Andrea Levy (b. 1956), Khaled Hosseini (b. 1965), have continued to help widen the curriculum. However, these texts are often still studied in the same, traditional way. What needs to change is the way we look at texts; new ways of looking, new ways of doing – and being – English.

In many respects, these are exciting times in which to live and to be doing English. It is in some small way, through developments in English, that people are beginning to see society from fresh viewpoints. This discipline more than any other, with its strange mix of literature, language, identity and tradition, is a crucible in which new versions of national identities are being formed. Through 'doing English' we understand ourselves and our identities afresh.

Summary

- English is intimately involved with questions about our national identity, as national identity is constructed culturally.
- Nations are communities which exist *in the imagination*, built upon by a shared stock of images, ideas, stories and traditions.
- Your national identity affects your ideas about yourself, your expectations, your relations with others and how others react to you. We are all both the *objects* created by national identity and the *subjects* who, in turn, create it. It is instilled into us and, in turn, performed by us.

- Those cultural things from the past which are chosen to shape the 'we' of the imagined community make up a 'cultural heritage'. Traditionally, English, the subject, is a form of cultural heritage, both in the texts it chooses (the canon) and in the way it interprets those texts.
- However, national identity is changing, both because it is clear that there never was one, single national identity and because we now inhabit a *hybrid* society. Both the books on English courses, and how we interpret them are changing to reflect this.

12

English, literature and politics

- What is politics, and what does English have to do with it?
- How does the study of literature become involved with issues of race and gender?
- How do different critical attitudes approach the issue of literature and politics?
- Why has English been a political battleground?

There has always been more to English than acquiring basic skills. In a book called *Bringing English to Order* (1990), Ivor Goodson and Peter Medway argue that 'English has been the means through which powerful groups, especially governments, have sought to achieve ends which were ... not neutrally "educational"'. They picture English as a 'battleground' where 'groups with agendas' clash. This is still true today and English as a subject has always been involved in political debates.

English and the *polis*

But what does politics mean in this context? Usually, when conversations turn to 'politics' they tend to be about the parties in power, the most recent or upcoming elections or the personal qualities of people whose job it is to be politicians. But politics is really about much more than that: the word comes from the ancient Greek word *polis*, meaning 'city', which hangs on in words like 'metro*poli*tan', 'Metro*polis*' and – as characters in *Men at Arms* (1993) by the British writer Terry Pratchett (b. 1948) point out – '*poli*ce officer' and '*poli*tician'. But it means much more than 'city', also denoting 'community' or, more widely, 'society'. Politics is about people, societies and how we live together, not just the events at Westminster, in Brussels or on Capitol Hill; the word covers an enormous area of human life. Of course, literature, too, is involved with people, societies and how we get along with one another. Dealing with the same issues in this way, literature and politics are inevitably bound together.

I have already shown how English was developed to mould people: a 'political' process. That process, although it was designed in the British colonies, is still functional today. Arguments that might appear to have a very limited relevance, about what should or shouldn't be read, about the canon, about how people should talk and write, or about assessment, are 'actually arguments about shaping . . . people's views of the world' (as two writers on the subject, Robert Protherough and Judith Atkinson, suggest in their contribution to Susan Brindley's *Teaching English* of 1994). Brian Cox goes further and is more specific in his 1995 book *Cox on the Battle for the English Curriculum*: 'control of the National Curriculum can lead to control of the way children think. A national curriculum in English influences attitudes to class and race.' Whether you think English as a subject is about personal growth, learning skills for the workplace or social world, understanding cultural heritage or offering cultural analysis, English is a very political subject, and all these things affect how we get along.

But English, as a subject, is perhaps even more closely involved with these debates about how we get along for the following reason: the study of literature is one of the very few subjects where individual experience is taken seriously as knowledge, as something you can learn about. Its hallmark is, as the critic Robert Young writes, the 'value and attention it gives to the personal and the subjective'. Other humanities subjects like history or geography do take account of what people say or write, but only as evidence for historical or geographical work. The knowledge they develop is about, say, the development of a country or the use of land in a city. In English, the knowledge is about the representation, form and content of the person's experience. Robert Young goes on: while, for example, there are 'plenty of histories of colonialism . . . such histories rarely considered the ways in which colonialism was experienced, or analysed, by those who suffered its effects'. The same is true of all sorts of issues. The novels of Dickens brought about a wide awareness of the plight of the London poor in the nineteenth century, and this led to some degree of political and social change. More recently, work that focuses on and takes seriously women's experience, represented in literary texts, has helped bring often hidden issues into the light, and into discussions of how we might live together.

However, sometimes our ways of reading make it hard to see these texts for what they are. For example, the issue of race, politics and literature has been very significant in the USA in the last thirty years or so. One of the first steps in understanding the representation of the African-American experience has been a re-evaluation of the canon. Just as the African critics I discussed in Chapter 5 argued that some Europeans thought African writing was not 'literary' but 'anthropo- logical . . . sociological, journalistic, topical ephemera', it was important to establish that much African-American literature was 'literary' and was a valuable source for thinking about the experience of being black in America. Indeed, it was to this tradition of African-American writing that US president Barack Obama (b. 1961) turned in trying to under- stand the complexities of race in America, and his own 'nightmare vision' of it. In his autobiography *Dreams from my Father*, he describes how he turned to the work of Langston Hughes (1902–1967), Richard Wright (1908–1960), James Baldwin (1924–87), W. E. B. DuBois (1868 – 1963) and Malcolm X (1925–1965), whose autobiography was written in collaboration with Alex Haley (1925–1992), who wrote the best-selling novel *Roots* (1976). The work of the ground-breaking African-American critic Henry Louis Gates took this argument a stage further. Aware that the more traditional ways of interpreting literary texts were very 'Western', that they had possibly questionable presuppositions which meant that they might not grasp the importance or key issues in African-American literature, he and others have developed an approach more suited to dealing with texts from this tradition. Gates focuses on the idea of 'signifying', which he sees as describing a way of reusing and recombining other texts to make a distinctive African-American way of seeing and engaging with the world and other people. As the experiences of African-Americans are expressed, and are properly valued and understood, he argues, the awareness of the need for wider political and social change will grow.

Looking back over this book, much of it has been about the relationship between the *polis* and English. I outlined, for example, how the 'canon' was a construction that reflected not just the need for a curriculum, but also political motives and ideas, and I showed how Shakespeare has been used for political purposes. Chapter 10 showed that English is involved with ideas about national identity and culture, and that some of the recent changes in English respond to changing ideas about national communities and identity. Rather than look at every aspect of this, as politics covers an enormous area, I shall examine the relationship between politics and the critical attitudes that influence ways of interpreting outlined in Chapter 4.

Critical attitudes and politics

Although politics and literature are interwoven, how the interaction actually works is still an open question. One way of looking at this is to refer back to the broad critical attitudes I discussed in Chapter 4. The *extrinsic attitude* moves from the text out to the context. It argues that literature is about the world and worth studying for what it tells us about the world. In contrast, the *intrinsic attitude* focuses on the text itself, its form and structure. It suggests that texts, especially 'great texts', have an ingrained artistic value and so are worth studying in their own right. These two attitudes lead to very different understandings of the relationship between politics and literature.

The extrinsic attitude: literature as politics?

Those who share the extrinsic attitude will have no problem explaining how literature is political. Since texts are about the world, then they will also be about how we get along – that is, about politics. Some critics show, for example, how texts display ideas about the politics of the time they were written or the political ideas of the author. If the ideas of the author are not of interest for interpretation, the extrinsic attitude might suggest that the 'voice of history' could be speaking through the text to reveal (without the author's knowledge) a range of taken-for-granted political ideas. Others, sharing this extrinsic attitude, will concentrate on how texts are used. One example of this is the cultural-materialist approach to Shakespeare, looking at the way 'Shakespeare' – both the plays and the institution – is a construct of present-day political, cultural and economic concerns. In this case, literature and ways of interpreting literature are seen as a political tool to be questioned, taken over or taken back. Where the political position of an approach or a text is hidden, the aim of the extrinsic critic is to uncover it.

Many of those who share the extrinsic attitude understand English to be 'cultural politics'. This is a rather catch-all term for thinking about the relationship between politics and culture. Politics – how we get along – exists in many different cultural spheres. There are national, regional and local politics, for example. Politics is also involved in different spheres of what people do and where they are. You might hear about the 'politics of the workplace', say, or 'the politics of the playground'. So culture, too, is political. As I suggested with the example of 'national culture', culture gives us our sense of who we are and how we should be. It is all to do with politics. Cultural politics, then, is where politics and culture are interwoven. For example, the canon, a 'cultural' idea, has political consequences. (Whose voices are we allowed to hear? What are they saying?) Conversely, a political idea, such as 'everyone should be equal', has cultural effects. (Would a film that argued that people shouldn't be equal be acceptable? Would it be successful?) 'Cultural politics' argues that politics is reflected in culture, and culture in turn reflects back and influences how we get along. If English is a version of cultural politics, then each text we study is a political event and every text tries to convince us of certain ideas about how we should get along.

Some people argue that doing cultural politics is the whole point of doing English. In education, this approach is sometimes known as 'critical literacy'. Wendy Morgan, in *Critical Literacy in the Classroom* (1997), argues that the job of teachers of English and literary critics is to explore and to uncover the 'assumptions that underwrite texts ... investigate the politics of representation, and ... interrogate the inequitable cultural positioning of speakers and readers'. Questioning assumptions is obviously vital, but following such a single explicit agenda might risk simply replacing 'one way of doing English' with another 'one way of doing English'.

The intrinsic attitude: literature versus politics?

In contrast, the intrinsic attitude implies a very different understanding of the interweaving between society and literature. For critics who share the intrinsic attitude, to see English as cultural politics is to miss the artistic worth, the 'literary-ness', of a work of literature. To do English is to concentrate on the special features that make a work of literature great art. It is wrong, from this point of view, to look at the sociology, polemical messages or social intent of a literary text. In this sense, they might argue, literature is *counter* to politics and to the way in which people use power.

This idea has come in for a great deal of criticism. It seems to imply that you could think about a text 'in a vacuum' separate from the world. It also implies that judgements about value can be unaffected by other opinions and ideas that you might have. For example, a work might offer a viewpoint about society with which you disagree completely, but you might still value it as a great work. Yet even this approach assumes that literature is involved in 'how we get along'. Indeed, if the power of literature lies in the ways in which experience is represented and structured, perhaps it is the 'great works of art' that do this most acutely. Some people who follow the 'intrinsic' attitude argue that literature 'teaches moral truths', or that it embodies the 'human spirit'. But you don't have to believe this to see that an art work can have an amazing, unpredictable and transformative effect on people's lives and situations. Exploring and perhaps fostering these, is, in the end, about 'how we get along', which is why studying literature is about politics in the widest sense.

Why has English been a political battleground?

The question remains: Why do politicians, teachers, academics, journalists and others argue so much over the subject of English? There are a number of reasons. Perhaps most importantly, ideas clash over English because, as both a popular and, in the UK, compulsory school subject, it is one of the larger forums in which many people encounter a structured approach to cultural issues. As I have suggested, cultural activity, especially education, plays a large role in shaping and controlling our ideas about such things as identity and social hierarchies, and has a huge influence over our world-views. Studying literature, as a part of culture in general, is a very powerful way of forming people, not least because it is there, most often and most clearly, that people's experience is represented. So, when people seek to shape ideas, to convince others and to make changes in society, the subject of English is one of the tools to which they turn.

This process of shaping and moulding has become even more important because we live in an age of mass communication, where the way we represent things has become much more significant. Think of the debate over the canon discussed in Chapter 5, for example. Including works by those who have traditionally been considered a minority (texts by African-American women, say) is a form of representation. Studying a wider range of texts offers a broader and more open representation of the world and, as a result, it also might help to prevent people from being excluded not only when we think about what 'literature' might be, but also when we think about what 'society' might be. Those with an interest in such issues have seized upon English as a forum for discussing their ideas.

English is also controversial because it is in many respects one of the most important subjects in education. This is not because knowledge about Shakespeare, for example, is more important than being able to do maths (because it isn't), but more simply because English teaches literacy and the interpretative skills on which the other subjects are based. It is rather like 'an under-labourer' providing materials and abilities which support a range of different disciplines. This key role means that if anybody – politicians, teachers, academics or the media – tries to change the education system as a whole, they must turn first to English. As Ivor Goodson and Peter Medway suggest, 'changing English is changing schooling'. As a result, English becomes both a 'test tube' for education policy and a 'weathervane', showing which ideas are strongest at any time in education as a whole. This could explain why those interested in education react very strongly to any proposed changes to English courses.

Doing English, then, makes us sensitive to 'how we get along', to the *polis*. To do English is to become involved with others, through literature and language. It leads you to uncover ideas other than your own and new ways of thinking about things. We might think of reading as a private, solitary activity, but all the time it is forming links between you and others in the world. Reading by yourself is, in fact, one of the most social, political activities you can do.

Summary

- Politics can be defined in its broadest sense as 'how we get along'. English, in dealing with literature, also deals with ideas about society and our place in the world. The two are inextricably linked, not least because of the way literature deals with the individual's experience.

- Those who support *extrinsic* forms of criticism suggest that texts are about the world, and that English is a form of 'cultural politics'; a point where politics and culture are interwoven. Those who support *intrinsic* criticism would disagree with this, but still acknowledge the link between literature and how we see our place in the world. Whether these critics realise it or not, this makes 'English' a political activity.

- English is a site of controversy, because it is an inherently political subject. Issues of representation within English courses are increasingly seen as important in the 'wider world', so the subject is a focus for those interested in such issues. As well as this, the interpretative skills taught in English are at the base of all other subjects, so anyone wishing to change education must engage with English.

13

Interdisciplinary English

- How is English linked to other disciplines?
- What are the consequences of this?
- English and science: a special case?
- Is English evolving?

English is interwoven with all the other subjects that we study. Just as other subjects cast light on English, English the subject, where we think about how we read, casts light on other subjects.

Diffuse, fuzzy and interwoven

I have argued that the subjects we study at school, college and university are inventions, *constructed* in certain times and places for certain reasons. Part of the point of this was to show that we 'make' knowledge by actively dividing and categorising the world. One effect of this is that every discipline, if you look at it hard enough, is fuzzy at the edges – for example, where does organic chemistry end and biology begin? The divisions are not clear-cut, because the world itself is not made up of clear-cut categories. Another effect is that disciplines are, for the most part, interwoven with each other. To study sociology, for example, you need to know about history, maths, statistics and so on. Of all the subjects we study, English is perhaps the most diffuse and interwoven and has the fuzziest edges of all.

English is like this perhaps because it is the subject closest to the shifting changes in ideas about 'how we get along'. I have shown in previous chapters how the choice of the literature we study is motivated by a range of factors, how authors are used to make political points and how the subject is involved with ideas about identity. There is nothing 'neutral' about English; it is very closely linked to people's ideas about the world and is used and changes accordingly. It is also fuzzy and interwoven because there is no fixed core to the subject: despite attempts over many years to enforce an idea of 'a right answer', there is nothing that is 'really English'. Moreover, although studying English teaches skills that are absolutely essential, none of these core skills are unique to English. Some people might argue that the 'intense study of the words on the page' – close reading – is the key skill in English, but lawyers and philosophers (for example) study phrases and words very closely and, in fact, anybody who needs to make a detailed, intelligent response to a text has to scrutinise it. Literacy and even a good writing style are both necessary for the study of all disciplines. Even the material studied is not unique to English. Historians read Shakespeare to get a point of view on Elizabethan and Jacobean life, for example, and geographers might read Shakespeare to find out how perceptions of space in general and places in particular have changed. Fuzziness also appears in the aims of English as a subject. Many teachers argue, perhaps rather vaguely, that English is about 'personal growth', meaning that it helps you to think about yourself and to develop your place in the world. But to study other subjects would provide this – learning about both history and psychology, as examples, would help you to understand where you fit into the world. Many also say that there is increasing overlap between disciplines: English gives to some disciplines, and takes from others.

What you learn in English can cast light on many other disciplines, and perhaps the clearest example of this is the relationship between English and history. There are obvious similarities between the two disciplines: literature is full of stories or *narratives*; history is constructed of narratives about the past. Both subjects rely on interpretation: in English you read and interpret texts; in history you read and study texts produced by historians ('history books') or texts produced within the period you are studying (documents). But the similarities do not end there. In English you learn that no interpretation can be 'neutral', so every history book, even the most 'factual' textbook, is full of taken-for-granted ideas, about, say, why things change in history or the role of women. Whether the author realises it or not, these have shaped her or his analysis of any particular historical event. Moreover, every history book is written in a particular style. A history book could be written in a style that tried to sound objective (most are), or in a style that tried to actively convince you of something (a polemical style). In this way, historical writing can be seen as another literary genre, bound by conventions and expectations, just like a play or a poem. Again, looking at how we read is as informative as what we read. Issues of interpretation, aired in English, offer a whole new understanding of the way history is studied.

By the same token, much of what you study in English, especially if you adopt the 'extrinsic attitude', derives from the discipline of history. But English also takes material and ideas from other disciplines – psychology, art history, religious studies, politics, sociology, women's studies and so on. For example, if you wanted to find out about the audience for a Dickens novel in the nineteenth century, you might be most successful reading books not about or by Dickens, but about Victorian society. English not only has no unique skills but it also draws upon perhaps all the other subjects you could study.

What are the consequences of this?

For all these reasons, English, more than any other subject, has no 'heartland'. It is an interdisciplinary subject, a rag-bag, a miscellaneous collection, from all over, rather than a subject in itself. This means that it is actually rather like the literature – the undefineable or uncategorisable category – that the subject aims to study. The fact that this has not become so clear in English at school, college and Access courses shows the continuing strength of the idea that there was a core to the subject and only 'one way' of doing English. This difficulty of definition has two consequences. First, it means that the subject you study is the most open to discussion, argument and change in its aims, methods and objectives. This controversy, whether it is by negotiation amongst experts, through obscure articles in learned journals, by violent argument in the media, or by government intervention in education, affects you. It is also an unending controversy: just as there is really no right answer to an essay question, there is no right way of laying out a programme for doing English as a subject. The second consequence of being a 'rag-bag' is that it does, in fact, put English in a special position. If the subject is not tied to a 'one way of doing' or to a 'right answer', those of us who study it should be free to investigate any number of exciting new ideas. All disciplines ask, to some extent, *how* they interpret and *how* they read their material. But it is in English that these key questions and central debates are – or should be – faced most clearly. In studying English we investigate and engage most with reading texts. In doing so we must engage most with the issues of interpretation that are vital to understanding those texts, ourselves and others.

English and science: a special case?

In talking about the close relationship between English and other disciplines, many people assume that this just means the arts or humanities subjects, because science is somehow 'different'. Certainly the relationship between English and the sciences has long been rather strained. Until now my discussion has used examples from the arts, but science and English do have common ground: both can be seen as subjects studying our place in the world.

In 1959, the physicist, novelist and scientific administrator C. P. Snow (1905–1980) gave the annual Rede lecture, in Cambridge. Its title was 'The Two Cultures and the Scientific Revolution' and its theme was the gulf of understanding between the arts and the sciences. Snow argued that, on the one hand, people in the arts (including those doing English) see scientists as uncultured, illiterate, amoral, unable to appreciate beauty and lacking in any understanding of the human condition. On the other hand, he said, scientists see those of an arts persuasion as missing out on the 'revolution of the age' and as backwards-looking intellectual snobs. He went on to state that 'arts people' know scandalously little about the science that shapes our world, ignorant even of the most basic principles. His example was the second law of thermodynamics. Knowing this, he said, is equivalent to having read a work by Shakespeare. 'Arts people' have all read at least one Shakespeare play, but none seem to know the second law of thermodynamics. (Do you?) But this ignorance of the world we all live in, he said, is hardly noticed, simply because science is not seen as being important. This gulf is a 'practical and intellectual and creative loss' to us all and does damage right through our society. Rather than bridging this gulf, however, Snow's well-meaning lecture appears to have made it wider. In response, F. R. Leavis gave a lecture in 1962 called 'Two Cultures? The Significance of C. P. Snow'. It had very little actual argument and amounts to little more than a roar of contempt (exactly the sort of 'snobbery' Snow expected, in fact). It was filled with extremely hostile abuse (one remark from many: Leavis wrote, 'Snow is, of course, a – no I can't say that: he isn't: Snow thinks of himself as a novelist'). Leavis ended by maintaining that English is the central discipline that most embodies 'perception, knowledge, judgement and responsibility'. In many respects, things have hardly changed since then.

But there were points on both sides of this argument. First, science plays an increasingly important role in everybody's life, both in technology and the machines we use everyday, and as a way of understanding the world. Perhaps the most significant example of this is the huge change in the way we understand ourselves after Darwin. His idea of evolution through natural selection challenged the most basic ideas about what it meant to be human. Where, before Darwin, the Western world had been dominated by the Christian idea of the creation of Adam and Eve, suddenly, after Darwin, we were human animals, evolved and evolving just like any other animal. In *Darwin's Dangerous Idea* (1995), the philosopher Daniel Dennett writes that this 'eats through just about every traditional concept, and leaves in its wake a revolutionized world view, with most landmarks still recognizable, but transformed in fundamental ways'. Yet, as the biologist Richard Dawkins (b. 1941) points out, 'the subjects known as the humanities are taught almost as if Darwin had never lived'. It seems strange that such a major change in world-view fails to influence a discipline as much about our world-views as English is supposed to be.

Second, it is clear that (as Snow suspected) the humanities and science can have a very constructive influence on each other. One attempt to cross this divide – from the science side – has been by Dawkins, whose book *Unweaving the Rainbow* (1998) points to the way science illustrates the beauty of the world and the cosmos. Rightly, Dawkins points out the shortsightedness of those who find science dull, dead and mechanical, or just 'don't like it'. Dawkins is not insisting, of course, that everybody becomes a scientist: just as you can enjoy music 'without being able to play a note on an instrument', you can appreciate science 'as something to read and rejoice in'. Science could even be seen as a literature of the wonder of the world. To those who think that science simply 'solves' the mysteries of the world, Dawkins argues that 'mysteries do not lose their poetry when solved. Quite the opposite: the solution often turns out to be more beautiful than the puzzle.' If science is the 'poetry of the universe', doing English could mean learning to appreciate this.

But the exchange is not just one way. Doing English can teach scientists as well – not about how to do science, of course, but about the role of science in the world. For example, even in *Unweaving the Rainbow*, Dawkins is strident in his pursuit of scientific truth and exposes many fakers and frauds. But he is also strident in his dismissal of other approaches to wider cultural issues that he considers. A case in point is Dawkins' reaction to the 'Kennewick Man', a 9000-year-old skeleton found in Washington State in 1996. As the scientists were beginning to do DNA tests on the remains, the five local Native American tribes demanded the return of the remains (which were exhumed on their land) for burial. Dawkins cites one as saying, 'from our oral histories, we know that our people have been part of this land since the beginning of time. We do not believe our people migrated here from another continent, as the scientists do.' Dawkins finds this laughable, and satirically suggests that the archaeological scientists declare themselves a religion in order to get the body back for analysis. The point here is not that science itself is right or wrong, but that this was a very sensitive issue, involving people's very deeply held beliefs. Thinking about the effects of science and seeing the case from another point of view – accepting a different interpretation of the facts – might be very important here. This is not to suggest that facts like the date of the body are invented, but that the importance of the facts lies in what you do with them. Science is only one part of culture and to interpret events 'only as a scientist', as it were, is to fail to take into account the complexities of the cultural situation. The scientific approach is one way of looking at or attending to the world, amongst others. Appreciating this, and allowing for different interpretations, might mean that even more serious versions of the Kennewick Man incident could be negotiated with respect for everybody.

Another way in which the ideas developing in English are important for science are made clear in Steven Roses's book *Lifelines* (1997). Here, he tells the 'Parable of the Frog'. Five biologists are having a picnic by a pool when they see a frog jump. They ask themselves why. One says that it is because the frog saw a snake, passed a signal from its brain to its legs and contracted its muscles to jump and escape. The second says that this process must be seen in a wider environmental context: the frog desires to avoid being eaten. The third points out that it can only jump because, as it grew up from a tadpole, it developed the muscles, nerves and so on to enable it to jump. A fourth argues that it jumped because, through evolutionary selection, its species had adapted to escape successfully from snakes. The final biologist takes a chemical view: the frog jumped because of a chemical reaction in its muscles ('interdigitated filamentous proteins, called actin and myosin'). None of these different interpretations of why the frog jumped – physiological, contextual, developmental, evolutionary and biochemical – are incorrect. But each depends on different presuppositions in the act of interpreting, as each biologist has a different interest and point of view. An awareness of the different ways in which interpretation can take place, of the different contexts and presuppositions – hermeneutics – is as important for science as it is for literary study.

Is English evolving?

These debates over English might seem a long way from you, as you study the subject at school, college or on Access courses. But everybody involved in the subject is caught up to some degree in these arguments. The responses people have already made to these debates have already shaped how you have done English and how you will be doing it in the future. For some, the interdisciplinary nature of English is seen as a threat; in a sense, they are caught in a paradox. On the one hand, they admit that the subject is woven in with others; on the other, they want to hold on to an idea that English is a discipline purely in its own right and has a special way of interpreting texts that has nothing to do with other subjects (usually the 'Leavis' method). Changes and threats to this, such as thinking about how we read, or reading a wider range of texts than in the past, are often opposed tooth and nail. Other people have a different response, and happily admit the interdisciplinary nature of English; they see this as a chance to change the subject and help it evolve.

English is already developing by analysing a wider range of sorts of text. Already, secondary teachers teaching pre-twentieth-century texts often show films or TV adaptations to their students, which widens the category of English. The relatively new discipline of *cultural studies* grew from precisely this interdisciplinary understanding of English. Where English traditionally looked at 'literature', cultural studies analyses all aspects of culture, from artworks (novels, poetry, plays, but also comics, films, TV programmes, music and so on) to other sorts of 'cultural production' (the design of houses, fashion) to social habits (going to nightclubs, being part of certain groups). All these are 'texts' to be interpreted. This new discipline also sets all these things in their social, political and historical context.

These sorts of changes, then, are responses to the understanding that how we read is as important as what we read. I have suggested that the study of English should make us confront these issues of interpretation clearly and in a direct way. Moreover, as the world we inhabit changes dramatically, it is becoming clear that learning 'facts', though important especially at earlier stages of education, is less significant than *learning how to learn* and *thinking about how facts and processes are generated.* Much business analysis (to cite one example from many, many others) is now concerned with *how* and *why* things appear, rather than what they are. If doing English means thinking about hermeneutics or how we interpret, it is a crucial way of learning how to engage with the modern world. Understanding the world around us means knowing what you are doing when you interpret it.

Summary

- The subjects we construct are interwoven with other subjects and never clear-cut. English is perhaps the 'fuzziest' – it is closest to the shifting changes in politics, because there is no 'right answer' and no unique, central skill in English. English also draws upon, but also feeds into, a very wide range of disciplines.
- All this means that English is the subject most open to discussion, argument and change. It also gives those studying English enormous freedom to explore new and changing ideas.
- English and the sciences have long seemed opposed, but they could benefit from one another. Science can help us to appreciate 'the poetry of the cosmos', while English can help us to be more culturally sensitive.
- English is still evolving. English continues to focus on enabling you to respond to the world around you.

Conclusion

The importance of English

This book is about *why* and *how* we do English. It is a book about ideas, ideas to be used as tools, and has explained what you are doing when you are doing English. The book has covered some key ideas for English today that have long been established in higher education and are now, gradually, becoming part of secondary education in the UK.

Many of the ideas I have described affect your assessment, exams, choice of texts, aims, objectives and everything else to do with English, usually without your knowing. I think it's important to see how and why things are done the way they are. (Ben Knights and Chris Thurgar-Dawson write suggestively that the 'history of a discipline is, among other things, a covert history of the relation between the culture of the staff tribe and that of the student tribe': part of the point of this book has been to uncover this secret history.) This is not least because, if you know why you are doing something, it makes it much more straightforward to do. As you progress in English, you will realise that I have simplified ideas and issues from time to time: because it's often assumed that everything you do in English should be 'naturally' accessible, simplification is often frowned upon. But again, this book is a tool or, to use a famous metaphor, a ladder to be thrown away after use. (You might begin the process of 'throwing it away' by thinking about what's wrong with the model of reading presented in Chapter 2.) I have no control over how anything in this book might be interpreted: it's up to you what you make of it. But isn't that the case with every text?

I have suggested that English is rapidly developing. It used to be the case that in order to succeed in the study of literature, students had to learn to look through one set of eyes, perhaps very different from their own. In doing so, they accepted, often without realising it, the world-view behind the 'English' that was developed as a subject in the first half of the twentieth century. Among other things, this turned potentially exciting literature into bland exam fodder. All this risked making English into a subject studied as a bland ritual, a 'heritage' subject, and ran roughshod over the fact that students at all levels come from different backgrounds, have different formative experiences and different presuppositions.

The situation has changed, however, and one sign of this change is the wider diffusion of new ideas and innovative ways of looking at literature, often through what is called 'theory'. Theory isn't just an arbitrary collection of names and jargon. Theory – as I've said, not a good term – stands for the new questions that readers ask of literary texts that weren't asked before (and so it reveals that older approaches have particular questions that they ask and issues that they pursue). We ask new questions because the world has changed and the need for new ways of thinking about it stems from that change. For example, we do not read feminist theory and criticism to play at being feminists: we read it because there are important questions to be asked about women's roles and lives, and about gender issues. We do not ask post-colonial questions to dress up as 'post-colonialists' while we teach or study these texts: we ask them because we all inhabit a post-colonial world and how we understand and live with the consequences of empire is important, as events all over the world clearly show. English – including theory – is not an abstract glass bead game played only for pleasure, it is a discipline that, through the study of literature, attempts to comprehend better the world around us and to appreciate the others that inhabit it. How we read is part of how we are in the world we share and questions about this arise from reading texts. Our reading and interpretation grows out of our experiences, concerns and hopes for ourselves and others.

Change has been quite slow, however. Strangely, even when 'theory' began to gain ground among academics, many in education still felt that students should be 'started off' with the more traditional approaches to English, then introduced to 'theory' if they should choose to take English to a higher (degree) level, as a sort of optional extra. In the UK, this resulted in a wide gap (some would say a yawning gulf) between the 'old'

English A level or equivalent and English in higher education 'This isn't what I expected: why are we doing this?' was a common question amongst first-year students of English literature. Of course the situation will differ from country to country, but many students notice 'gaps' in approach from one course to the next, or even from one module to the next, depending on the views of the lecturers or the people who create and examine the courses. Problems will always remain, but what is really important is that you, the students, need to know how and why the problems have arisen.

This book, then, has sought to look at some ideas that shape the study of literature today and in this way to answer the 'why are we doing this' of those adjusting from 'traditional' to 'theoretical' ways of doing English.

To summarise:

- English deals with texts, certainly, but not just with what we read. It also explores *how we read*. It is concerned with the *interpretation* of texts and ideas that arise from interpretation. The French writer and thinker Michel de Montaigne (1533–1592) wrote that 'we need to interpret interpretations more than we interpret things', and *how we interpret* texts, whether they are novels, TV advertisements, political speeches (or anything), is absolutely central to the world today. More-over, exploring how we read is also 'learning about learning' and so adds to a wider range of skills and ideas that will continually develop through life. The expertise in interpreting texts and thinking about interpretation that you learn from English may be applied in other fields.
- Once we are aware of different ways of interpreting texts, it becomes clear that there is *no neutral, objective approach* to literature. In turn, this means there could be no single method of doing English, new or traditional, and no single correct interpretation. I feel that we should watch out for replacing 'one way of doing English' simply with 'another way of doing English'. English is a pluralist subject (it accepts a wide range of approaches) and is open-ended – 'doing' English is never 'done'.
- Because of its development and content, English is a *very diffuse* subject. In one sense it is an 'under-labourer' to other disciplines; not just because it teaches skills of literacy, writing and reflection, but because it examines interpretation, which is vital for other subjects on

the curriculum. But English is also a subject where a huge range of ideas is played with, constructed, taken apart, argued over and so on. It reflects the infinite scope that literature displays, and should, perhaps, demonstrate this flexibility more frequently. A consequence of this 'diffuseness' is the endless controversy surrounding English. Because the subject has no one obvious core, everybody with an agenda wants to claim that the particular issues that concern them are central to English.

• English, as culture and as a subject that studies culture, is *involved with our relationships with others and with the world*. Culture is woven inextricably into how we get along and has far-reaching effects in the wider world. A consequence of this is that English is not just about texts, but also about you, about others and about the nature of society.

• None of this is to argue that in English 'anything goes'. Looking at texts, interpretation and a wide range of significant ideas, then relating this to our cultures and societies, involves knowledge and careful thought. Perhaps most of all it involves constantly taking *responsibility* for each interpretation. English also asks: *Why* do you think that about the text?

Nearly all education has two sides to it. One is about learning skills and facts for their own sake, proving you have them by passing exams and getting a qualification, which in turn opens doors. The other side to education is much vaguer and is about fulfilling your own potential, following your own interests, exploring yourself and others, your society, the world, and becoming – often in some indefinable way – a better person. But just because these aims sound vague and you couldn't be assessed on them does not mean that they are not valuable. In fact, some might say that these are truly the point of education. Nearly forty years ago, the late Harold Rosen, a leading commentator on education, stressed precisely this side of the subject of English: it is

> nothing less than a different model of education: knowledge to be made, not given; knowledge comprising more than can be discursively stated; learning as a diverse range of processes, including affective ones; educational processes to be embarked on with outcomes unpredictable; students' perceptions, experiences, imaginings and unsystematically acquired knowledge admitted as legitimate curricular content.

This is stirring: but there are exams, too. However, sometimes the assessment side and the fulfilment side of education run together and the whole process can be a joy. Sometimes – more often, perhaps – they don't, and 'getting the right answer' kills off all the indeterminate but very real interest. Theory, with its concern to offer different ideas and different voices and to validate different approaches, is, among other things, part of an attempt to bring these two sides together again.

Moreover, while the 'moral mission' of English turned out to be an illusion – subtly coercing people to share the views of a certain type of person of a particular class, colour, sex and of a certain age – there is a link between the study of literature and ethical responsibility. Many people argue that the all-encompassing ideas and systems that led people to take some central beliefs for granted have collapsed or are in the process of collapsing. For example, even if we choose a system by which to orientate ourselves – a set of political beliefs, religious beliefs or a philosophical approach to the world – we have usually actively chosen it, rather than just simply accepted it, as people in the past might have done. The result of this is that each of us is more *responsible* in two ways. First, decisions, especially decisions about doing the right thing, have to be argued and negotiated, even though there may be no absolute surefire way of proving them 'correct'. The burden of this now falls on each of us, not on a system of beliefs to which we adhere. Second, and because of this, we have to be sensitive enough to *respond* to each situation and each choice as best we can. This involves not just viewing the situation as fully as we are able, but also reflecting on the ideas and approaches that led to that particular interpretation. And English as a subject has a role to play here, in making us more reflective and responsive.

Some people argue that literature shows us other people's experience, or that it teaches us to 'walk a mile in somebody else's shoes'. This experience, they suggest, makes us more responsive to other people's needs, ideas, hopes and fears. The trouble with this idea is that, even after reading a book or poem that does this (and of course not all do, or are interpreted as doing so), it is still possible to forget, or to assume that this one story is only a story. Walking a mile in somebody's shoes is walking only a mile, and a sensitivity can soon become calloused again. Our responsiveness is perhaps better developed by thinking about *how* we read. By understanding different presuppositions and by uncovering what we take for granted, it is possible to develop a habit of constantly questioning whatever you read or see or think or do. This constant questioning in turn develops a heightened responsiveness.

You, as a reader and student of English, should be free to explore many methods of interpretation, or to hop from one to the other, or to experiment with a selection. By consciously seeking out and using different methods of interpretation, motivated by presuppositions different to our own, each of us can bring to light, learn about and, perhaps, challenge our own preconceived ideas. This leads to ideas about works of literature that are new, interesting and exciting in themselves, but also helps us to see the world differently. In this way the power of literature is clear: it can continue to unsettle us and to make us question even our most closely held beliefs, not only about art but also about ourselves, others, society and the wider world.

The philosopher Hannah Arendt (1906–1975) celebrated what she called 'natality', the interruption into life of birth. She goes on:

> The new beginning inherent in birth can make itself felt in the world only because the newcomer possesses the capacity of beginning something anew, that is, of acting. In this sense of initiative, an element of action, and therefore of natality, is inherent in all human activities.

Indeed, it is this possibility of unpredictable newness, fully experienced, that bestows 'faith and hope upon human affairs'. And it is this sense of 'unpredictable newness', really, in that part of 'human affairs' that involves literature, its reading, writing and interpretation, that this book has been about. English is a contested and constantly evolving discipline. New ideas, new books, poems and plays, new ways of reading and writing and the new demands these make create its unpredictable newness. No one knows what will happen next, and we have to strive to be open to what we can't yet know. This means that the future – of the subject, of how we understanding literature, of literary creation – lies with you, the active reader, now, doing English.

Further reading

They say that students, teachers and academics are just the reproductive system of libraries – after all, each one recreates a little library. If this is true, then the DNA of libraries is encoded in bibliographies. A bibliography serves two purposes: to show where the ideas you have been reading about came from and to provide a list of further things to read. This bibliography aims mainly to serve the second of these purposes (though all the critical works I have cited are mentioned here). It offers a 'first port of call' for what to read next. Most bibliographies have a mixture of books and journal articles, but this contains mainly books, because they are more easily accessible.

Introduction

It's hard to find a book that sums up English. The cult (and excellent) American writer David Foster Wallace (1962 –2008) puts it like this:

'Critical appreciation' means having smart, sophisticated reasons for liking whatever literature you like, and being able to articulate those reasons for other people, especially in writing. Vital for critical appreciation is the ability to 'interpret' a piece of literature, which basically means coming up with a cogent, interesting account of what a piece of lit means, what its trying to do to/for the reader, what technical choices the author's made in order to achieve the effects she wants and so on. As you can probably anticipate, the whole thing gets very complicated and abstract and hard, which is one reason why entire college departments are devoted to studying and interpreting literature.

For a sense of doing English, at a tangent and with tongue in cheek, try:

- David Lodge, *Nice Work* (1989), *Small World* (1984) and *Changing Places* (1975), anthologised together in a *David Lodge Trilogy* (London: Penguin, 1993)
- Fay Weldon, *Letters to Alice, on First Reading Jane Austen* (London: Sceptre, 1993)

A good introduction to a range of literature and to contemporary ideas is:

- Richard Jacobs, *A Beginners Guide to Critical Reading* (London: Routledge, 2001)

For those interested in the specific challenges of 'transition' from secondary to higher education and on the relation of AS/A to Higher Education, the English Subject Centre has these really useful reports, available online, from the (http://www.english.heacademy.ac.uk/)

- David Ellis, *Report 17: In at the Deep End? The First Year in Undergraduate English Literature* (2008)
- Andrew Green, *Report 10: Four Perspectives on Transition: English literature from sixth form to university* (2006)

1 Where did English come from?

There is a growing number of books on the history and origins of English as a subject. An excellent account of the early history of English and on the current AS/A2 levels is

- Carol Atherton, *Defining Literary Criticism* (Basingstoke: Macmillan, 2005)

Other important studies include:

- Chris Baldick, *The Social Mission of English Criticism, 1848–1932* (Oxford: Clarendon Press, 1983)
- Brian Doyle, *English and Englishness* (London: Routledge, 1989)
- Gauri Viswanathan, *Masks of Conquest: Literary Study and British Rule in India* (New York: Columbia University Press, 1989)

E. M. W. Tillyard offers a personal account of the development of the subject in *The Muse Unchained* (London: Bowes and Bowes, 1958), and Bernard Bergonzi's book, *Exploding English: Criticism, Theory and Culture* (Oxford: Clarendon Press, 1990) is an entertaining, polemical, personal history of English from the 1950s to the 1980s. Henry Nettleship's pamphlet is *The Study of Modern European Languages and Literatures in the University of Oxford* (Oxford: Parker, 1887). Other documents in relation to this, including selections from the Newbolt Report and Collins, can be found in: *Writing Englishness 1900–1950*, edited by Judy Giles and Tim Middleton (London: Routledge, 1995) and *The Origins of Literary Studies in America*, edited by Gerald Graff and Michael Warner (London: Routledge, 1989).

Robert Crawford, in a number of acute studies, helps nuance the story of the development of English by exploring how the discipline was established and developed in Scotland, in part as a kind of 'internal colonialism'. See Robert Crawford (ed.), *The Scottish Invention of English Literature* (Cambridge University Press, 1998). There is also an account of English in a European context in *European English Studies: Contributions towards the History of a Discipline* ed. Balz Engler and Renate Haas (Leicester: The English Association, 2000).

Other studies include:

- Harry Blamires, *A History of Literary Criticism* (London: Macmillan, 1991)
- Gary Day (ed.), *The British Critical Tradition: A Re-evaluation* (Basingstoke: Macmillan, 1993)
- D. J. Palmer, *The Rise of English Studies* (London: Oxford University Press/Hull University Press, 1965)
- Peter Widdowson (ed.), *Rereading English* (London: Methuen, 1982)

There is also a website on the 'History of English Studies' at www.english.ucsb.edu/faculty/rraley/research/englstud.html

There is also a great deal of material on the Leavises, including a very good biography by Ian MacKillop, *F. R. Leavis: A Life in Criticism* (London: Penguin, 1997), and studies by:

- Michael Bell, *F. R. Leavis* (London: Routledge, 1988)
- Gary Day, *Re-reading Leavis: Culture and Literary Criticism* (Basingstoke: Macmillan, 1996)
- Francis Mulhern, *The Moment of Scrutiny* (London: New Left Books, 1979)
- Anne Samson, *F. R. Leavis* (London: Harvester Wheatsheaf, 1992)

Leavis's texts are well worth dipping into. Not only are they historically interesting, but also they often make extremely acute critical points and are excellent examples of close reading. The most interesting include: F. R. Leavis, *New Bearings in English Poetry* (1932), *Revaluation* (1936), *The Common Pursuit* (1952), *The Great Tradition* (1948) and *The Living Principle* (1975). Most of these have been reprinted recently by Penguin. In the same vein, I. A. Richards, *Practical Criticism* (London: Routledge & Kegan Paul, 1973), originally published in 1929, is perhaps the seminal book in the development of close reading. William Empson, *Seven Types of Ambiguity* (London: Penguin, 1995), originally published in 1930, is a masterpiece of this genre, and Wayne Booth, *The Rhetoric of Fiction* (London: University of Chicago Press, 1961), is also extremely accessible.

Other texts, interesting for themselves as well as being key for the development of English, are Matthew Arnold, *Culture and Anarchy*, edited by J. Dover Wilson (Cambridge: Cambridge University Press, 1960), and T. S. Eliot's influential essays, including 'Tradition and the Individual Talent', in his *Selected Prose*, edited by Frank Kermode (London: Faber and Faber, 1975). Harder to find is Eliot's infamous, arguably racist and antisemitic *After Strange Gods* (London: Faber and Faber, 1934 – never reprinted).

The image of the 'Chinese encyclopedia' is from Borges and was also very memorably used by the French philosopher and historian, Michel Foucault (1926–1984), in his influential and complex book *The Order of Things* (London: Tavistock/Routledge, 1970).

2 Doing English today

There are a number of introductions to 'literary theory' and English today. These are among the best:

- Andrew Bennet and Nicholas Royle, *An Introduction to Literature, Criticism and Theory* (London: Pearson, 2004) is a very interesting, innovative introduction to key critical concepts.
- Peter Barry, *Beginning Theory: An Introduction to Literary and Cultural Theory* (Manchester: Manchester University Press, 2002)

Clear, coherent and aimed specifically at AS and A2 level students is

- Adrian Beard, *Text and Contexts* (London: Routledge, 2001)

A very useful source book for teachers is

- Jane Ogborn and Lucy Webster with Barbara Bleiman, *Text, Reader, Critic: Introducing Context and Interpretations* (London: The English and Media Centre, 2000)

There are also a number of general 'textbooks' for English, with practical exercises and an emphasis on teaching. The best and clearest of these is:

- Rob Pope, *The English Studies Book*, 2nd edition (London: Routledge, 2002)

Other introductions include:

- David Ayres *Literary Theory: A Reintroduction* (Oxford: Blackwell, 2008)
- Hans Bertens, *Literary Theory: The Basics* (London: Routledge, 2001)
- Jonathan Culler, *Literary Theory: A Very Short Introduction* (Oxford: Oxford University Press, 1997)
- Terry Eagleton, *Literary Theory*, 3rd edition (Oxford: Blackwell, 2008). This best-selling 'introduction to theory' first edition was first published in 1983 and, although a new edition was produced in 2008, there were almost no changes, so it now looks very dated.
- Paul Goring, Jeremy Hawthorn, Domhnall Mitchell *Studying Literature: The Essential Companion* (London: Arnold, 2001)

- M. A. R. Habib *Modern Literary Criticism and Theory: A History* (Oxford: Blackwell, 2008)
- Chris Hopkins, *Thinking about Texts* (London: Palgrave, 2001)

There are two sorts of technical terms that English as a subject uses. The first sort are simply descriptive. (It's easier to say 'duple verse' or 'iambic verse' than 'verse that goes "du-dum du-dum du-dum du-dum"'.) The second sort are terms that implicitly present a wider critical approach. Each set of critical terms brings with it its own presuppositions and ideas, and many different approaches use many different terms (although some do overlap). In general, these terms actually work in the same way as the more descriptive terms (it is easier, say, to use 'reification' or 'objectification' – after explaining them, of course – than to repeat 'the processes of thought that turn people and abstract concepts into things'). Some people say that English (especially literary theory) has too much 'jargon'. Of course, anything which overuses technical terms is off putting. But simply to oppose technical terms, or the sophisticated ideas about literature they embody, assumes that there could be a 'natural' way of interpreting that does without a 'technical language' of any sort. It also assumes that doing English should be easier than a subject like chemistry or sociology, where technical terms abound. Two useful glossaries of these terms are:

- M. H. Abrams, Geoffrey Harpham *A Glossary of Literary Terms*, 9th Edition (Boston: Wadsworth, 2009)
- Jeremy Hawthorn, *A Concise Glossary of Contemporary Literary Theory* (London: Arnold, 2000)

The best introduction to the technical questions of meter and rhythm is:

- Derek Attridge, *Poetic Rhythm* (Cambridge: Cambridge University Press, 1995)

There are also a number of readers that have selections from major critics and theorists. One of the most wide-ranging is Julie Rivkin and Michael Ryan (eds), *Literary Theory: An Anthology* (Oxford: Blackwell, 2004). A different approach is taken by Peter Brooker and Peter Widdowson, *A Practical Reader in Contemporary Literary Theory* (London: Prentice Hall/Harvester Wheatsheaf, 1996), which apples theories to specific texts.

Patricia Waugh (ed.) *Literary Theory and Criticism: An Oxford Guide* (Oxford: Oxford University Press, 2006) is a really useful collection of original essays which cover a whole range of theoretical approaches to literature.

English is also very well served with websites. Here are just five relevant ones, at the time of writing:

* The English Server at http://eserver.org/
* The Voice of the Shuttle at http://vos.ucsb.edu/
* The Internet Public Library Online Literary Criticism Collection at http://www.ipl.org/ref/litcrit/
* The Humbul Humanities Hub at http://www.humbul.ac.uk/ – this is a really useful gateway site.
* The Literary Encyclopedia at http://www.LitEncyc.com/

The survey of English departments is: Council for College and University English, *The English Curriculum: Diversity and Standards: A Report Delivered to the Quality Assurance Agency* (1997). There is also a more recent English Subject Centre report by The Halcrow Group with Jane Gawthrope and Philip Martin *Survey of the English Curriculum and Teaching in UK Higher Education (Report Series 8)* (2003) (again, it's online), which, in this context, offers a similar picture.

Ben Knights's excellent article 'Intelligence and Interrogation: The identity of the English student' *Arts and Humanities in Higher Education* 4(1) 33–52 offers a really insightful view of changing nature of the English student in Higher Education.

3 English and 'the right answer'

English is one of the most-discussed subjects in the curriculum. Here are just a selection of the books that reveal the mechanics of how English is taught, and why it's taught the way it is.

Anything by Brian Cox is worth reading for a sense of the relationship between the government, the subject and the educational institutions, especially *Cox on Cox: An English Curriculum for the 1990s* (London: Hodder & Stoughton, 1991) and Brian Cox, *Cox on the Battle for the English Curriculum* (London: Hodder & Stoughton, 1995).

Sections of this chapter draw heavily upon Patrick Scott's excellent (but now a bit dated) book *Reconstructing A-level English* (Buckingham: Open University Press, 1989).

On the new AS/A2 criteria are

- Adrian Barlow, *Second Reading* (Leicester: The English Association, 2005)
- June Blunkett, Susan Cockcroft, Ann Harris, John Hodgson, Gary Snapper *Text: Message: The Future of A Level English* (Sheffield: NATE, 2004)
- *English 21: Playback* (London: QCA, 2005) (available online)

Other books in this area include:

- Martin Blocksidge (ed.), *Teaching Literature 11–18* (London: Continuum, 2000)
- Susan Brindley (ed.), *Teaching English* (London: Routledge, 1994)
- Brian Cox (ed.), *Literacy is not Enough: Essays on the Importance of Reading* (Manchester: Manchester University Press/The Book Trust, 1998). This is a wide-ranging and stimulating collection on the importance of literature and its teaching.
- Wendy Morgan, *Critical Literacy in the Classroom* (London: Routledge, 1997)
- Harold Rosen, *Neither Bleak House nor Liberty Hall: English in the Curriculum* (London: Institute of Education, 1981). Dated now, but a sterling statement of principles.
- Chris Searle, *None but our Words: Critical Literacy in the Classroom and Community* (Buckingham: Open University Press, 1998). Just what it says, it's idealistic and rather inspiring.

Interesting on 'nuts and bolts' is M. T. Fain, *An Investigation into the Effect of Question Choice in A-level English* (Aldershot: AEB for General Certificate in English, 1975). The title describes it excellently. Its astounding conclusion?

Students are most likely to choose the questions on which they will get the highest marks. In effect, this means you answer questions for which there is most institutional support in terms of TV productions to watch, passnotes and websites to revise from and so on. Question choice reaffirms the canon.

There are also a number of journals that deal with this field. Especially good is *Changing English*.

The Qualifications and Curriculum Authority website is at http://www.qca.org.uk

4 Critical attitudes

René Wellek and Austin Warren's ideas about intrinsic and extrinsic are developed in *Theory of Literature*, 3rd edition (Harmondsworth: Peregrine, 1963), one of the most famous New Critical discussions of what literature is.

5 Literature, value and the canon

The question 'What is literature?' has exercised writers, critics and philosophers for a very long time. Places to start might be:

- Aristotle's *Poetics* is short and straightforward. Try it, you'll be surprised.
- Plato, *The Republic*, Books 2, 3 and 10. This is one of the earliest and most influential discussions of literature and, in these sections, is not too hard or too long.

More recent attempts to answer the question include René Wellek and Austin Warren's *Theory of Literature* (see above, under Chapter 4), where they outline their understanding of the issues. Derek Attridge's excellent and clear *The Singularity of Literature* (London: Routledge 2004) offers a very interesting and innovative account of the literary. Jonathan Culler outlines a very different answer in his *Structuralist Poetics* (1975). There is a challenging, but fairly accessible, discussion of literature by Jacques Derrida, one of the most influential contemporary thinkers, in an interview, 'This Strange Institution Called Literature', in Jacques Derrida, *Acts of Literature*, edited by Derek Attridge (London: Routledge, 1992). Imre Salusinszky, *Criticism in Society* (London: Routledge, 1987), has a number of interesting and accessible interviews with critics about literature and criticism. Rob Pope's *The English Studies Book* (see above, under Chapter 2) is also a good place to start. Henry Louis Gates Jr, *Loose Canons: Notes from the Culture Wars* (Oxford: Oxford University Press, 1992) is very accessible indeed, with the funniest discussion of the canon available.

Again, the canon is a subject that has generated a great deal of controversy. In addition to the Leavis and Eliot material already mentioned, this is a small selection of accessible books on the subject:

- Harold Bloom, *The Western Canon* (London: Macmillan, 1995)
- Alastair Fowler, *Kinds of Literature* (Oxford: Clarendon Press, 1982)
- John Guillory, *Cultural Capital* (London: University of Chicago Press, 1993)
- Robert von Hallberg (ed.), *Canons* (London: University of Chicago Press, 1984)
- Barbara Herrstein Smith, *Contingencies of Virtue* (London: Harvard University Press, 1988)
- Frank Kermode, *The Classic* (London: Harvard University Press, 1983)
- Robert Scholes, *Textual Power* (London: Yale University Press, 1985)

The citation from Chinweizu, Onwuchekwa Jemie and Ihechukwu Madubuike comes from *The Decolonization of African Literature* (Washington: Howard University Press, 1983). Toni Morrison is quoted from 'Unspeakable Things Unspoken: The Afro-American Presence in American Literature', *Michigan Quarterly Review* 27(1) (1989): 1–34. Brian Cox is cited from *Cox on the Battle for the English Curriculum* (see previously, under Chapter 3).

6 Doing Shakespeare

Here is just a very small selection of books relevant to the debates outlined in this chapter:

- Katherine Armstrong and Graham Arkin, *Studying Shakespeare: A Practical Guide* (London: Prentice Hall, 1998)
- Jonathan Bate, *The Genius of Shakespeare* (London: Picador, 1997)
- Jonathan Dollimore and Alan Sinfield (eds), *Political Shakespeare: New Essays in Cultural Materialism* (Manchester: Manchester University Press, 1985)
- Malcolm Evans, *Signifying Nothing: Truth's True Contents in Shakespeare's Texts* (Harvester: Brighton, 1986)

- Rex Gibson (ed.), *Secondary School Shakespeare: Classroom Practice* (Cambridge: Cambridge Institute of Education, 1990)
- Terence Hawkes, *Meaning by Shakespeare* (London: Routledge, 1992)
- Terence Hawkes, *That Shakespeherian Rag: Essays on a Critical Process* (London: Methuen, 1986)
- Graham Holderness (ed.), *The Shakespeare Myth* (Manchester: Manchester University Press, 1988). This includes David Hornbrook's article, '"Go Play, Boy, Play": Shakespeare and Educational Drama'.
- Susan Leach, *Shakespeare in the Classroom* (Buckingham: Open University Press, 1992)
- Sean McEvoy, *Shakespeare: The Basics* (London: Routledge, 2000)
- Kiernan Ryan, *Shakespeare*, 3rd edition (Basingstoke: Palgrave, 2002)
- Gary Taylor, *Reinventing Shakespeare: A Cultural History from the Restoration to the Present* (London: Hogarth Press, 1989)

The quotations from Fay Weldon are in *Letters to Alice, on First Reading Jane Austen* (see previously, under Introduction), pages 11–20. Ludwig Wittgenstein discusses Shakespeare in *Culture and Value* (Oxford: Blackwell, 1998 edition). The article by John Yandell is 'Reading Shakespeare, or Ways with Will', in *Changing English* 4(2) (1997): 277–294, and the James Wood review is 'To See or not to See', *Guardian*, 12/13 October 1994. The citation from Swinburne is from the general introduction to *The Complete Works of Shakespeare* edited by Edward Dowden (London: Henry Froud/Oxford University Press, 1910).

'New Historicists' and 'Presentists': James Shapiro is the author of the widely celebrated *1599, A Year in the Life of William Shakespeare* (London: Faber and Faber 2005). Among Stephen Greenblatt's many stylish and readable books are *Hamlet in Purgatory* (Princeton: Princeton University Press, 2001) and *Will in the World: How Shakespeare became Shakespeare* (London: Jonathan Cape, 2004). An admirable introduction is *Stephen Greenblatt* is by Mark Robson (London: Routledge, 2008). Terence Hawkes edits a collection called *Shakespeare in the Present* (London: Routledge, 2002) as well as a series called 'Accents on Shakespeare' from Routledge which explores all sorts of new angles in this field. Ewan Fernie writes powerfully on 'Shakespeare and the Prospect of Presentism', too, in *Writing about Shakespeare (Shakespeare Survey 58)* ed. Peter Holland (Cambridge: Cambridge University Press, 2005): I've quoted from both of these. Fernie, too, with Simon Palfrey, edits a series of short, accessible and polemical books called *Shakespeare Now!* There's a blog: http://shakespearenowseries.blogspot.com/. These books also relate to what I say in the final section of Chapter 10.

It would be fair to say that writing on Shakespeare has led to some of the most beautiful and interesting critical prose: a really good example is the very moving and perceptive introduction by Jonathan Bate to a new edition of Shakespeare's *Complete works: the RSC Shakespeare* eds Jonathan Bate and Eric Rasmussen (Basingstoke: Macmillan, 2007).

7 The author is dead?

The essays to which I refer are: Roland Barthes, 'The Death of the Author' (equally interesting and perhaps more useful is his essay 'From Work to Text'), Michel Foucault 'What is an Author?' and W. K. Wimsatt and M. C. Beardsley, 'The Intentional Fallacy'. All these, and a great deal more relevant material, are included in an excellent reader edited by Seán Burke, *Authorship from Plato to the Postmodern* (Edinburgh: Edinburgh University Press, 1995). Burke has also written two very good studies of this issue, critical of the 'death of the author' idea: *The Death and Return of the Author* (Edinburgh: Edinburgh University Press, 1992) and *The Ethics of Writing* (Edinburgh: Edinburgh University Press, 2008). An outstanding, if demanding, account of these issues of authorial intention is Kaye Mitchell, *Intention and Text* (London: Continuum, 2008). Andrew Bennett discusses the author interestingly and clearly in *The Author* (London: Routledge, 2005).

8 Metaphors and figures of speech

Perhaps the most significant and accessible recent work on metaphor has been carried out by George Lakoff and Mark Turner, sometimes in collaboration. Many of the ideas and examples in this chapter are drawn from their work. Especially good, and highly recommended, is *More than Cool Reason: A Field Guide to Poetic Metaphor* (London: University of Chicago Press, 1989). Other works include George Lakoff and Mark Johnson, *Metaphors We Live By* (London: University of Chicago Press, 1980), and George Lakoff's *Women, Fire and Dangerous Things: What Categories Reveal About the Mind* (London: University of Chicago Press, 1987). Also interesting on this is a reader edited by Deborah Cameron,

The Feminist Critique of Language (London: Routledge, 1998 edition). More complex, but very rewarding, is Jacques Derrida's essay, 'White Mythology: Metaphor in the Text of Philosophy', in *Margins of Philosophy* (London: Harvester, 1982). Slightly at a tangent to all this, but still about the power of language, is J. L. Austin, *How to Do Things with Words* (1962). This is a very famous and influential account of language use. At the beginning he writes that 'What I shall have to say here is neither difficult nor contentious', and – amazingly – that's (mostly) true. It's not long, either.

9 Narrative and closure

There is a great deal of material on narrative and narratology, but less on closure. A very good starting point is H. Porter Abbot's *Narrative* in the Cambridge Introduction series (Cambridge: Cambridge University Press, 2002). Shlomith Rimmon-Kenan's *Narrative Fiction: Contemporary Poetics* (London: Routledge, 1990) is exhaustive but (perhaps) a little dull. An excellent selection of key texts, which covers previous developments like Propp, as well as new ideas on this topic is *The Narrative Reader*, edited by Martin McQuillan (London: Routledge, 2000). The best example of 'narratology' in full flow is Gérard Genette, *Narrative Discourse*, trans. Jane E. Leavis (Oxford: Blackwell, 1980). A more demanding but worthwhile book on narrative is Peter Brooks, *Reading for the Plot: Design and Intention in Narrative* (London: Harvard University Press, 1992). Frank Kermode's oblique, beautiful and significant book on closure *The Sense of an Ending* has been reprinted recently (Oxford: Oxford University Press, 2000).

10 Creative and critical rewriting

A good, clear guide for students is:

- Steve May, *Doing Creative Writing* (London: Routledge, 2007): it seeks – in my words – to orient, equip and encourage students of creative writing.

There is a growing list of books that explore or argue over creative writing and its role in English. Some of these I have referred to in the chapter.

- Ben Knights and Chris Thurgar-Dawson's *Active Reading: Transformative Writing in Literary Studies* (London: Continuum, 2006) is an insightful book, from which I have drawn much. It offers a clear argument about the importance of innovative practice in teaching English, and an array of examples and case studies. Its aim is to fill the 'woeful gap between the sublime theoretical possibilities and the actual teaching practice' in English analysed by Rob Pope in his 1995 *Textual Intervention: Critical and Creative Strategies for Literary Studies* (London: Routledge, 1995).

- Michelene Wandor's *The Author is not Dead, Merely Somewhere Else: Creative Writing Reconceived* (Basingstoke: Palgrave Macmillan, 2008) is a polemical and slightly fragmented book, full of striking judgements, though too few to make the 'reconceived' in the title accurate.

- D. G. Myers *The Elephants Teach: Creative Writing Since 1880* (Chicago: University of Chicago Press, 2006) is a rewarding history of the history of creative writing, mainly in the USA. The title comes from a remark made when the novelist Vladimir Nabakov (1899–1977) was offered a chair (a Professorship) in literature at Harvard: the famous linguist Roman Jacobson (1896–1982) asked 'what next? Shall we appoint elephants to teach zoology?'

- Paul Dawson, *Creative Writing and the New Humanities* (London: Routledge, 2005) is also a history and an argument about the subject, concluding that the creative writer is in a position to be a radical public intellectual.

- Rebecca O'Rourke, *Creative Writing: Education, Culture and Community* (Leicester: NIACE, 2005) is another history, with a UK focus, with a strong sense of what creative writing is for.

- *Creative Writing Studies: Practice, Research and Pedagogy* edited by Graeme Harper and Jeri Kroll (Clevedon: Multilingual Matters, 2008) is an up-to-date account of many of the debates within creative writing.

- The English Subject Centre, too, has a really helpful report by Siobhán Holland, *Creative Writing: A Good Practice Guide* (*Report Series 356*) (2003).

There is an academic journal dedicated to creative writing, called *New Writing: The International Journal for the Practice and Theory of Creative Writing* edited by Graeme Harper.

Angela Carter's comments come from *Shaking a Leg* ed. Jenny Uglow (London: Chatto and Windus, 1997), one of the best and most interesting collections of non-fiction by a twentieth-century British novelist, which it is a joy simply to browse through. The fantastic Facebook *Pride and Prejudice* is at http://www.much-ado.net/austenbook/. Douglas Cowie's first novel is *Owen Noone and the Marauder* (Edinburgh: Canongate, 2005): it's great, I read it non-stop in one night. Geoffrey Hartman's words come from his *Criticism in the Wilderness* (New Haven: Yale University Press, 1980): his own creativity is described in his autobiography *A Scholar's Tale* (New York: Fordham University Press, 2007).

11 English, national identity and cultural heritage

This is a huge and growing area. One of the most important books here is Benedict Anderson, *Imagined Communities: Reflections on the Origin and Spread of Nationalism*, revised and extended edition (London: Verso, 1991). Another cultural critic, Stuart Hall, has much to say on this and related issues of gender and ethnicity. See, for example, Stuart Hall and Paul Du Gay (eds), *Questions of Cultural Identity* (London: Sage, 1996) and his discussion in *Critical Dialogues in Cultural Studies*, edited by David Morley and Kuan-Hsing Che (London: Routledge, 1996). The work of Homi Bhabha is often hard, but very rewarding: see his edited collection *Nation and Narration* (London: Routledge, 1990), or his more challenging essays, *The Location of Culture* (London: Routledge, 1994). I quote from an essay called 'DissemiNation: Time, Narrative and the Margins of the Modern Nation', which appears in both these. Salman Rushdie's reflections in *Imaginary Homelands: Essays and Criticism 1981–1991* (London: Granta Books, in association with Penguin, 1991) are also very illuminating (the citation from Rushdie is from an essay called 'In Good Faith'). For a collection of documents about Englishness, see Judy Giles and Tim Middleton (eds), *Writing Englishness 1900–1950* (see previously, under Chapter 1). For linked accounts of similar issues, see the groundbreaking work by the critic Edward Said, including his justly celebrated *Orientalism* (London: Panteon Books, 1978) and its follow-up, *Culture and Imperialism* (London: Vintage, 1994). Also very illuminating in this area is the work of Paul Gilroy, especially his *Between Camps: Nations, Cultures and the Allure of Race* (London: Penguin, 2000) which refuses to duck any of the hard issues that these debates generate and *After Empire* (London: Routledge, 2004).

A key work introducing the idea of 'heritage' is David Lowenthal's *The Past is a Foreign Country* (Cambridge: Cambridge University Press, 1985). It has a follow-up in his book, *The Heritage Crusade and the Spoils of History* (Cambridge: Cambridge University Press, 1998). The quotation from Brian Cox appears in Susan Brindley, *Teaching English* (see previously, under Chapter 3).

12 English, literature and politics

The citations from Robert Young come from his exhaustive *Postcolonialism: An Historical Introduction* (Oxford: Blackwell, 2001). Edward Said also writes very interestingly on politics, especially in his collection, *The World, The Text and The Critic* (London: Faber and Faber, 1984). Wendy Morgan is cited from *Critical Literacy in the Classroom* (see previously, under Chapter 3).

Henry Louis Gates develops his ideas in his edited volume *Black Literature and Literary Theory* (London: Methuen, 1984) and in detail in *The Signifying Monkey: a Theory of Afro-American Literary Criticism* (Oxford: Oxford University Press, 1988). Other writers discussing the same issues are Cornel West (there is a good *Cornel West Reader* (New York: Basic Civitas Books, 1999)) and bell hooks. hooks's work is very accessible: her groundbreaking volume is *Ain't I a Woman: Black Women and Feminism* (London: Pluto, 1982) and of her later collections of essays, *Teaching to Transgress: Education as the Practice of Freedom* (London: Routledge, 1994) is a rewarding read in this context.

Literary criticism in the United Kingdom has a powerful, explicitly left-wing political strand. However, two figures stand out as particularly influential.

The first is Raymond Williams, and two good places to start with his work are:

- *Culture and Society 1780–1950* (London: Hogarth Press, reprinted 1990)
- *Keywords: A Vocabulary of Culture and Society* (London: Croom Helm, 1976)

A detailed introduction to his work is John Higgins, *Raymond Williams: Literature, Marxism and Cultural Materialism* (London: Routledge, 1999).

The second major left-wing critic is Terry Eagleton. In addition to his now rather dated *Literary Theory* (above), other useful books by him include *Ideology: An Introduction* (London: Verso, 1991), *The Significance of Theory* (Oxford: Blackwell, 1990) and his *After Theory* (London: Penguin, 2004): almost a sequel to *Literary Theory* and is oddly titled, since it argues that 'theory' is far from finished and we are not 'after it'. There is also the *Eagleton Reader*, edited by Steven Regan (Oxford: Blackwell, 1998) and a book on his work by James Smith: *Terry Eagleton* (Cambridge: Polity 2008).

13 Interdisciplinary English

The very best introduction to current debates about the way history and literary studies interact is Keith Jenkins, *Rethinking History* (London: Routledge, 2003). Other accounts of the importance of narrative for history include the beginning of Hayden White's excellent (if massive and complex) *Metahistory* (London: Johns Hopkins University Press, 1973).

The 'two cultures' debate can be found in C. P. Snow, *The Two Cultures and a Second Look* (Cambridge: Cambridge University Press, 2001) with a really astute introduction by Stefan Collini and in F. R. Leavis, *Two Cultures? The Significance of C. P. Snow* (London: Chatto and Windus, 1962).

Accessible or 'popular' science is also a huge and important field. In the field of life science, Richard Dawkins, especially his *The Selfish Gene*, new edition (Oxford: Oxford University Press, 1989), is an excellent place to start. Also outstanding are Daniel Dennett, *Darwin's Dangerous Idea* (London: Penguin, 1995) and *Consciousness Explained* (London: Penguin, 1991). Dawkins' *Unweaving the Rainbow* (London: Allen Lane, 1998) discusses art at some length, as this chapter suggests. A very good counterpoint to Dawkins, and to some of the more inflated claims of popular science is Steven Rose, *Lifelines* (London: Penguin, 1997).

At the time of writing, you can follow the continuing Kennewick Man story at http://www.tri-cityherald.com/kman/

Good introductions to cultural studies are:

- J. Storey (ed.), *Cultural Theory and Popular Culture: A Reader* (Hemel Hempstead: Harvester Wheatsheaf, 1994)

- Susan Bassnett (ed.), *Studying British Cultures: An Introduction* (London: Routledge, 1997)
- Dick Hebdige, *Subculture: The Meaning of Style* (London: Routledge 1979). A classic cultural studies text and extremely accessible.

Conclusion

Hannah Arendt is cited from *The Human Condition* (London: University of Chicago Press, 1998). Simon Swift's *Hannah Arendt* (London: Routledge, 2008) is a great introduction to her work for literature students.

Most of the books above discuss the significance of literature, English and criticism. Excellent places to begin reading in more detail about this are a short and very accessible essay by the American philosopher, Richard Rorty, 'Heidegger, Kundera, Dickens', in his *Essays on Heidegger and Others: Philosophical Papers, Vol. 2* (Cambridge: Cambridge University Press, 1991), and his very accessible book, *Contingency, Irony and Solidarity* (Cambridge: Cambridge University Press, 1989).

Index

Related titles from Routledge

Doing Creative Writing
Steve May

What is creative writing? How, and why, is it done?

Creative writing is one of the fastest growing areas of study, essential to disciplines such as English, drama, journalism and media. Aimed at prospective students and those beginning creative writing courses, *Doing Creative Writing* provides the ideal introduction to studying creative writing at university.

This immensely readable book will:

- equip students for study, summarising what to expect a creative writing course to offer, and so encouraging confidence
- orientate the reader in the field by explaining exactly what is 'done' when we 'do' creative writing
- offer inspirational advice to help get started – and practical advice about how to get the most out of the course as it progresses.

Doing Creative Writing draws on the input of students and their views of what they wish they had known before starting creative writing courses, along with the experience of teachers and writers themselves. It also contains a preface by Stephanie Vanderslice demonstrating the global growth of the discipline and the relevance of this book. Steve May's refreshingly clear explanations and advice make this volume essential reading for all those planning to 'do creative writing'.

ISBN 13: 978–0–415–40238–5 (hbk)
ISBN 13: 978–0–415–40239–2 (pbk)
ISBN 13: 978–0–203–93982–6 (ebk)

Available at all good bookshops
For ordering and further information please visit:
www.routledge.com

Related titles from Routledge

Critical Theory Today
Second Edition
Lois Tyson

This new edition of the classic guide offers a thorough and accessible introduction to contemporary critical theory. It provides in-depth coverage of the most common approaches to literary analysis today: feminism, psychoanalysis, Marxism, reader-response theory, new criticism, structuralism and semiotics, deconstruction, new historicism, cultural criticism, lesbian/gay/queer theory, African-American criticism and postcolonial criticism.

The chapters provide an extended explanation of each theory, using examples from everyday life, popular culture and literary texts; a list of specific questions critics who use that theory ask about literary texts; an interpretation of F. Scott Fitzgerald's *The Great Gatsby* through the lens of each theory; a list of questions for further practice to guide readers in applying each theory to different literary works; and a bibliography of primary and secondary works for further reading.

This book can be used as the only text in a course or as a precursor to the study of primary theoretical works. It motivates readers by showing them what critical theory can offer in terms of their practical understanding of literary texts and in terms of their personal understanding of themselves and the world in which they live.

Both engaging and rigorous, it is a 'how-to' book for undergraduate and graduate students new to critical theory and for professors who want to broaden their repertoire of critical approaches to literature.

ISBN 13: 978–0–415–97409–7 (hbk)
ISBN 13: 978–0–415–97410–3 (pbk)

Available at all good bookshops
For ordering and further information please visit:
www.routledge.com